BUNGALOW PLANS

Bungalow plans

BUNGALOW PLANS

Christian and Christen Gladu

Gibbs Smith, Publisher
Salt Lake City

First Edition

06 05 04   5 4 3

Published by

Gibbs Smith, Publisher

P.O. Box 667

Layton, Utah 84041

Orders: (1-800) 748-5439

www.gibbs-smith.com

Edited by Suzanne Gibbs Taylor

Designed and produced by Woodland Studio

Printed and bound in Korea

Library of Congress Cataloging-in-Publication Data

Gladu, Christian.
Bungalow plans / Christian Gladu and Christen Gladu.— 1st ed.
p. cm.
ISBN 1-58685-147-0
1. Bungalows—Designs and plans. 2. Architecture, Domestic—Designs
and plans. 3. Architecture—United States—20th century—Designs and
plans. I. Gladu, Christen. II. Title.
NA7571 .G59 2002
728'.373'0973—dc21
                            2001008049

CONTENTS

ACKNOWLEDGMENTS

WE WOULD LIKE TO THANK the following individuals for their help in putting together this book:

Henry Sayre

Scott Gilbride

Christian Delmar Martin

Karen Cammack

David Spellman

Irv Spellman

Jerry & Trisha Reese

Ruth Gothenquist

Mindy Miller

Al Tozer

Charlie Wenzlau

Eric Lewtas

Tom Tanner

Tim Ashmore

Mike & Debbie Schubert

Bob Moore

Lucia & Robert Knight

Stephen Bobbitt

Steve Erickson

John Robinson

Mike & Robyn Knoell

David & Beth Balas

Mike & Mary Adams

Ellen Wixted

Frank Renna

Suzanne Gibbs Taylor

WE WOULD ALSO LIKE TO THANK all of the homeowners who let us into their homes to bring you these wonderful plans.

PHOTO CREDITS

Randy Allbritton: The Winslow

David Balas: Phillips Residence

Stephen Bobbitt: Bobbitt Studio/Garlow

Stephen Bray of 4D Solutions: Craftsman Guest Cottages

Karen Cammack, Cammack Photography: The Erickson Manzanita, The Grey Hawk, The Birch, The Cherry, Schubert Residence, Milwaukee Garlow, NorthTown Woods Garlow, The Sonora, The Wilshire

Ross Chandler, Chandler Photography: House on the Hill, Bend Bungalow, The Tamarack

Scott Gilbride: The Plinth

Ruth Gothenquist: Rendering for the bungalow anatomy

Art Grice: Midden Point—The Wenzlau Residence, The Agate Pass

Robert Knight: The Cottage

Eric Lewtas: The New England Craftsman

Christian Delmar Martin: The Tumalo, The Hodges Manzanita, The Erickson Manzanita, The Birch, The Cherry, The Winslow, Schubert Residence, Milwaukee Garlow, NorthTown Woods Garlow, The Sonora

Robert Moore: House in the Woods

Nellie Sanger & Shelly Stock: Winthrop House

INTRODUCTION

When we build, let us think that we build forever. Let it not be for present delight nor for present use alone. Let it be such work as our descendants will thank us for; and let us think as we lay stone on stone, that a time is to come when those stones will be held sacred because our hands have touched them, and that people will say as they look upon the labor and wrought substance of them, "See! This our parents did for us."
—John Ruskin

HAVE YOU EVER STROLLED down a beautiful tree-lined street filled with uniquely detailed homes that seem to grow from the landscape, and sensed true harmony between things man-made and natural? Have you been in a room that embraces nature and extends its living spaces to the outdoors? Have you been to a place where neighbors cannot help but share a hello or a cup of morning coffee on a gracious front porch? If so, you have experienced the bungalow.

The bungalow, popularized nearly a century ago for its simplicity, informality, and commonsense approach to life, has lain dormant in the hearts of America for fifty years. America's yearning for the reinvention of home has revived the bungalow and the lifestyle it represents. But simply reproducing the bungalow unchanged from its original appearance would ignore the lessons we have learned and deny how our culture has evolved. Transcending architectural styles, the bungalow has evolved into a philosophical statement of how families live their lives and how houses have become homes. The homes featured in this book illustrate how designers, homeowners, and builders have reinterpreted the bungalow philosophy for the future.

The bungalow revival is in full swing, with designers and builders creating a new legacy of homes and communities for generations to cherish. Crafting a new bungalow is the synthesis of nature, family, design, and craftsmanship. The bungalow, with its emphasis on handcrafted beauty, quality workmanship, and respect for nature and materials, exemplifies how the most accomplished ordinary effects can equal a sum much greater than its parts. The bungalow is enjoying a renaissance and is appreciated by a new generation of homeowners with fresh enthusiasm and innovative ideas. Morris and Stickley's philosophy of respect for the beauty of fine craftsmanship and reverence for natural materials is as relevant today as it was a century ago.

HISTORY

HENRY M. SAYRE
DISTINGUISHED PROFESSOR
OREGON STATE UNIVERSITY
—CASCADES

⋮ IN OCTOBER 1901, Gustav Stickley, a forty-three-year-old furniture maker from Syracuse, New York, published a new magazine that he called *The Craftsman*. As its cover made clear, its inspirations were English. Its motto was from Chaucer—"The lyf so short the craft so long to lerne"—and its feature article was dedicated to the life and work of the English designer William Morris, whose firm, Morris and Co., was famous for its fabrics, wallpapers, carpets, furniture, stained glass, and ceramic tiles.

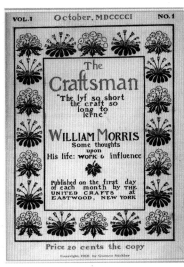

Stickley deeply admired Morris's design ethic. Morris claimed that the chief purpose of the designer was to elevate the circumstances of the common man. "Every man's house will be fair and decent," Morris wrote, "all the works of man that we live amongst will be in harmony with nature . . . and every man will have his share of the *best*." Such sentiments reflected Morris's appreciation for the writings of John Ruskin, whom Stickley also admired and who had died the year before *The Craftsman* was first published. Ruskin had argued, in what is perhaps his most famous essay, "On the Nature of Gothic," that the values of a culture are reflected in its architecture and design. He saw in the architecture of the Gothic era—not only in its cathedrals but in its cottages as well—a near-perfect relation between the craftsman and his work. Here was a work created in a condition of harmony, and Ruskin thought this ideal should guide all manufacturing and architecture.

Ruskin's essay was published in 1892 by Morris, and Stickley dedicated the second issue of *The Craftsman* to Ruskin as well. From Ruskin's philosophy, both men developed a common set of assumptions about how best to give "every man . . . his share of the *best*."

⋮ Every element of design, from the single chair to the entire home, must be honest to its materials.

⋮ It should be in harmony with nature, and should reflect what Morris called "the simplicity of nature."

⋮ It should be useful, functional, and durable.

⋮ It should be beautiful, but its beauty should derive from honesty, utility, and formal clarity, not from any "mis-applied ornament."

Stickley saw only one shortcoming in Morris's approach: The Arts & Crafts tradition that Morris epitomized relied too heavily on skilled handcraftsmanship, resulting in goods not generally affordable to the middle class. Stickley knew he had to rely on machine and mass manufacturing. When he published an article in December 1903 by Harvey Ellis entitled "How to Build a Bungalow," his idea was to spread the idea of the Craftsman home across the continent. Ten years later, he followed that with *Craftsman Homes: A Book for Home-Makers*, a book of bungalow designs (see below) meant to be filled with Stickley's Craftsman furniture.

From the beginning, the bungalow was conceived as a form of domestic architecture available to everyone. It was democratic. From Stickley's point of view, it embodied "that plainness which is beauty." The hand-hewn local materials—stone and shingles—employed in the construction tied the home to its natural environment. And so did its porches, which tied the interior to the outside, and which, with their sturdy, wide-set pillars, bespoke functional solidity.

Anyone familiar with the Prairie style of Frank Lloyd Wright will recognize in the description above the same principles that informed Wright's domestic architecture in the first decade of the twentieth century. Wright spoke of the Prairie house as "of" the land, not "on" it. Like the bungalow, it was to be constructed of local materials. His interiors were to be simple and plain, and as a result he usually designed his own furniture. "Simple things," he later said, "were nowhere at hand. A piece of wood without a molding was an anomaly." And though he eschewed the use of pillars for his porches, relying instead on the new technology of steel-reinforced cement cantilevers, he conceived of the porch as precisely "middle ground," the architectural link between the interior living space and the exterior environment.

Whether Wright influenced the bungalow tradition, or the bungalow tradition Wright, is impossible to say. What is clear is that they both helped formulate the fundamental architectural spirit of the first years of the century. There were

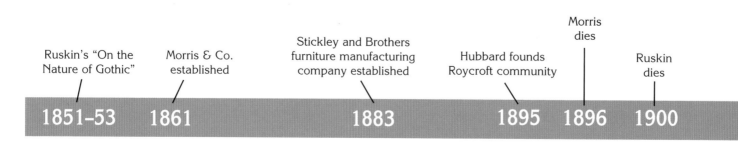

Ruskin's "On the Nature of Gothic"	Morris & Co. established	Stickley and Brothers furniture manufacturing company established	Hubbard founds Roycroft community	Morris dies	Ruskin dies
1851–53	1861	1883	1895	1896	1900

THE PHILISTINE

also many others who contributed to the movement. Just a few hundred miles from Stickley's Syracuse headquarters in East Aurora, New York, Elbert Hubbard, as early as 1895, had organized an Arts & Crafts community called Roycroft. Stickley and Hubbard shared many of the same designers, hiring skilled craftsmen away from one another. And Hubbard, like Stickley, published a magazine, *The Philistine*, far more utopian than Stickley's *Craftsman*, and more generally philosophical and political.

4580. Beautiful Bungalow Home, San Diego, Cal.

On the West Coast, architects Charles and Henry Greene, whose stated ambition was to create the "ultimate bungalow", championed the bungalow. Charles had seen Stickley's furniture at the 1902 Pan-American Exposition in Buffalo, and subscribed to *The Craftsman* soon after. Stickley, in turn, published pictures and plans of the Greenes' designs in his magazine, praising them for their ability to design homes "in which practical comfort and art are skillfully wedded."

By 1916, *The Craftsman* had ceased publication. A year earlier, Elbert Hubbard had died as a passenger on the ill-fated *Lusitania*. Greene & Greene dissolved their firm in 1922, but the bungalow movement was still all the rage. Bungalow building kits were marketed widely, and as many as 100,000 stock plans were sold by both national architectural companies and local lumber and building firms through the late 1920s. Across America, bungalows popped up everywhere. If the quality of these new stock bungalows could never match Stickley's best, let alone Greene & Greene's "ultimate" designs, they still aspired to a certain harmony of detail and solidity of construction. In the popular imagination, the word "bungalow" was synonymous with "quality." However, the Great Depression and then the Second World War spelled the end of the bungalow era. By the time the housing economy was refueled in the late 1940s and early 1950s, a new form of bungalow had emerged. Stripped of all refinement of spirit, all harmony with nature, the ranch house was born.

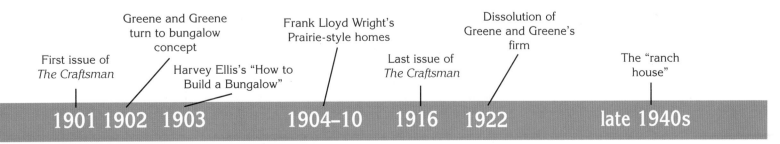

| 1901 | 1902 | 1903 | 1904–10 | 1916 | 1922 | late 1940s |

First issue of *The Craftsman*

Greene and Greene turn to bungalow concept

Harvey Ellis's "How to Build a Bungalow"

Frank Lloyd Wright's Prairie-style homes

Last issue of *The Craftsman*

Dissolution of Greene and Greene's firm

The "ranch house"

BUNGALOW ANATOMY

"I would rather be able to appreciate things I cannot have than to have things I am not able to appreciate."
—Elbert Hubbard

: TRADITIONALLY THE AMERICAN BUNGALOW is a one- to one-and-a-half-story structure with the narrow side of the home oriented toward the street. The half to full front porch identifies the main entry to the home. Original bungalow plans were simple in nature while still having an air of formality about them. Kitchens were isolated from dining rooms, which made them utilitarian work centers. Occasionally plans would include a built-in breakfast nook that would serve as the primary eating location in smaller one- and two-bedroom bungalows or as an auxiliary eating location in larger homes that included dining rooms. Built-in buffets and walk-through pantries served as connections from the dining area to the kitchen. Dining rooms were generally located in the center of the home, providing privacy from the street while still being conveniently adjacent to the kitchen, which was often located at the rear of the home. In climates where basements were common, stairs to the basement were adjacent to the kitchen to allow the basement to serve as an extension to the pantry. Living rooms were connected to dining rooms, and entrances were framed with either a *cased opening* or detailed columns and bookcases. The living room usually housed the fireplace, which was likely centered in the room and flanked by two high windows and built-in bookcases. Smaller bungalows often entered directly into the living room from the front porch; however, if the home were a larger one-story or one-and-a-half-story bungalow it would possibly have a distinct entry. These bungalows used the front entry to begin the staircase to the second floor, and stairs to the second floor would terminate in an upstairs hallway. Often two or three bedrooms and one bath would be located on the second floor. In some areas of the country, an outdoor *sleeping porch* was common on the first or second floor. In single-story bungalows, two to three bedrooms often surrounded a single bathroom. Many one- and two-story bungalows would have a study or *inglenook* located on the first floor adjacent to either the living or dining rooms.

Aesthetically, the bungalow is identified by large *overhangs*, lower-pitched roofs, *exposed eaves, roof brackets*, and multiple siding materials. The porch column bases anchor the home to the ground with the use of indigenous rock, brick, or stucco.

Upper porch columns were usually made from wood and are either tapered or constructed of exposed timber. Porches tend to be several steps up from the walkway,

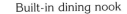
Built-in dining nook

shingles. In areas where basements were not prevalent and homes were built on post and pier systems, the siding would likely extend directly down to a concrete footing or just cut short of the grade line. In the eave of a single-story bungalow or in the gable or shed dormer of a one-and-one-half-story bungalow the siding material would change to shingles or shakes. *Gable ends* were often used for venting in warmer climates with the incorporation of screened openings that were embellished with horizontal and vertical lattice-work. On larger bungalows first- and second-floor materials may be separated with a horizontal *belly-band*, serving as a visual and physical transition between materials. Barge rafters were often detailed with individually designed *rafter tail* cutouts. Common rafter tails were left exposed to highlight the roof structure. *Shadow boards* were sometimes used to highlight the prominent barge rafter. Barge rafters sometimes appear to float outside of the building except where they are supported by *roof brackets*, which support the bottom edge of the rafter. Roof brackets vary in design and are key elements in identifying the bungalow style. In cases where a bungalow has an extremely low-pitched roof or for aesthetic reasons, an *outrigger* may be used to support the barge rafters. Outriggers generally are window headers that are run from the inside of the house and cantilevered outside to support the barge rafter.

elevating the porch from the street level. Chimneys are built outside of the building and are constructed of brick and native materials. The masonry column bases and chimney act as an anchor tying the building to the site. Landscaping enhances the building's base and reinforces the bungalow's connection with nature. The main floors of traditional bungalows were often separated from the foundation with a horizontal *water table* that worked as a base to begin the first-floor siding, which was usually comprised of siding or cedar

The bungalow style was by nature a less formal and more flexible architectural style and translated well to the craftsmen who built the original homes. Many homes were built from mail-order blueprints or featured designs in national periodicals. The plans were simple in most cases.

The extent of the architectural drawings consisted of only a wall section and exterior elevations that suggested materials and locations. Local craftsmen improvised and made their design modifications based on available materials, local building traditions, and environmental conditions. Unlike colonial architecture, the philosophical roots of the bungalow movement pre-dated the renaissance and in the spirit of the designer, craftsman bungalows were detailed and embellished on-site by their creators. The bungalow movement was blessed with invaluable designers such as Greene & Greene, Stickley, and home-production companies such as Sears, Montgomery Ward, and Aladdin Homes; however, the backbone of the bungalow style was the builders and artisans who interpreted details and materials into regional variations of the bungalow style and unknowingly developed an architectural style that was reflective of the people and the time.

Boxed beams

Mantel

Masonry fireplace

Built-in bookcases with or without glass doors

INTERIOR ANATOMY

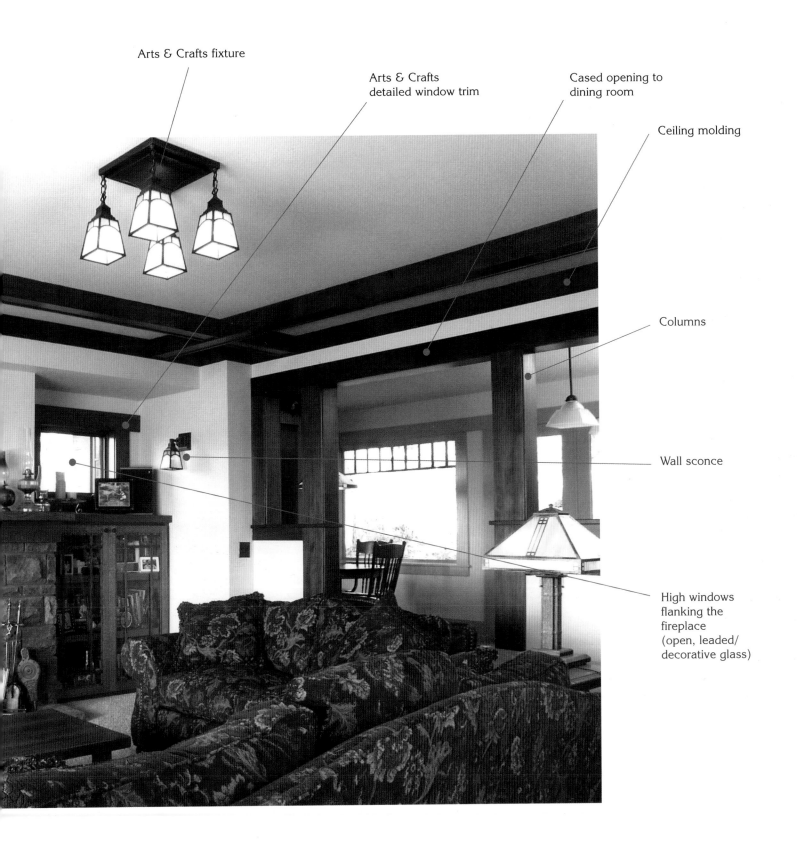

Arts & Crafts fixture

Arts & Crafts
detailed window trim

Cased opening to
dining room

Ceiling molding

Columns

Wall sconce

High windows
flanking the
fireplace
(open, leaded/
decorative glass)

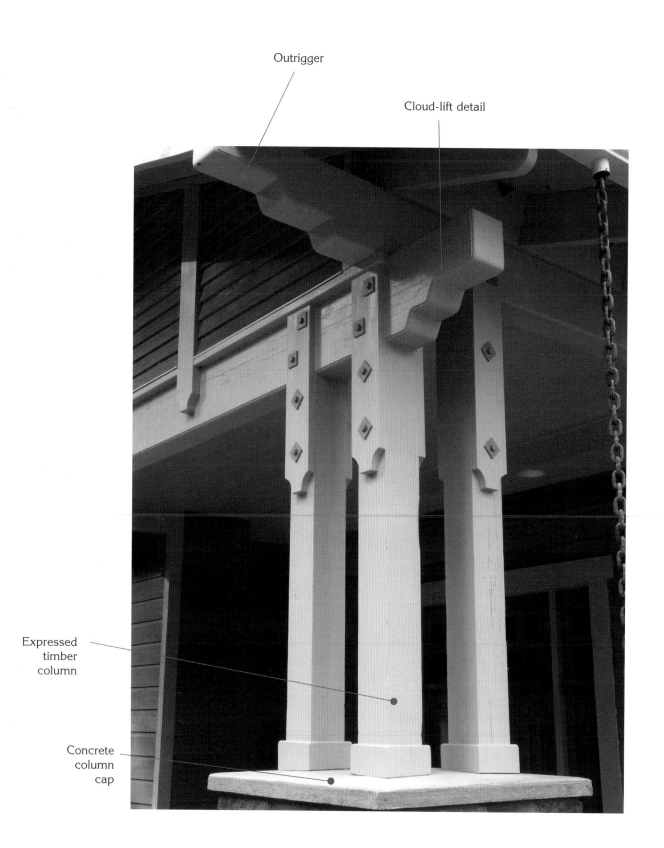

Outrigger

Cloud-lift detail

Expressed
timber
column

Concrete
column
cap

Building Costs

■ ■

: Home building is not an exact science; every builder and craftsman brings to the trade their own preferred way of building and estimating their work. A common question from potential homebuyers is "how much does a home cost per square foot?" This is a reasonable question since many realtors sell homes by volume and lending institutions appraise homes in part by applying a value per square foot. The reality is all 1,500-square-foot homes cannot be built for the same price. Home builders who repeatedly build the same home at the same quality level will tell you that the cost per square foot will vary on each home depending on site condition, weather, and lumber prices. New homes are not unlike automobiles in the sense that when you purchase a new car the price is not determined by the size of the car as much as the options and the complexity to build and deliver. Certainly cost per square foot is a good way to get started when creating a budget, but getting down to specifics is the only way to accurately estimate the cost of a new home. A good general rule is that the smaller the home, the more it will actually cost per square foot because every home has common core elements, such as kitchens, heating systems, and bathrooms. The cost of these big-ticket items will be spread over fewer square feet, bumping up the cost per square foot. The positive side to this equation is the fewer feet you build, the fewer feet you buy. Complexity of design site conditions and material specifications have a tremendous impact on what a home will cost. This is where consumers need to understand what they are buying and builders need to understand what the consumer expects prior to quoting ballpark square-footage prices.

■ ■

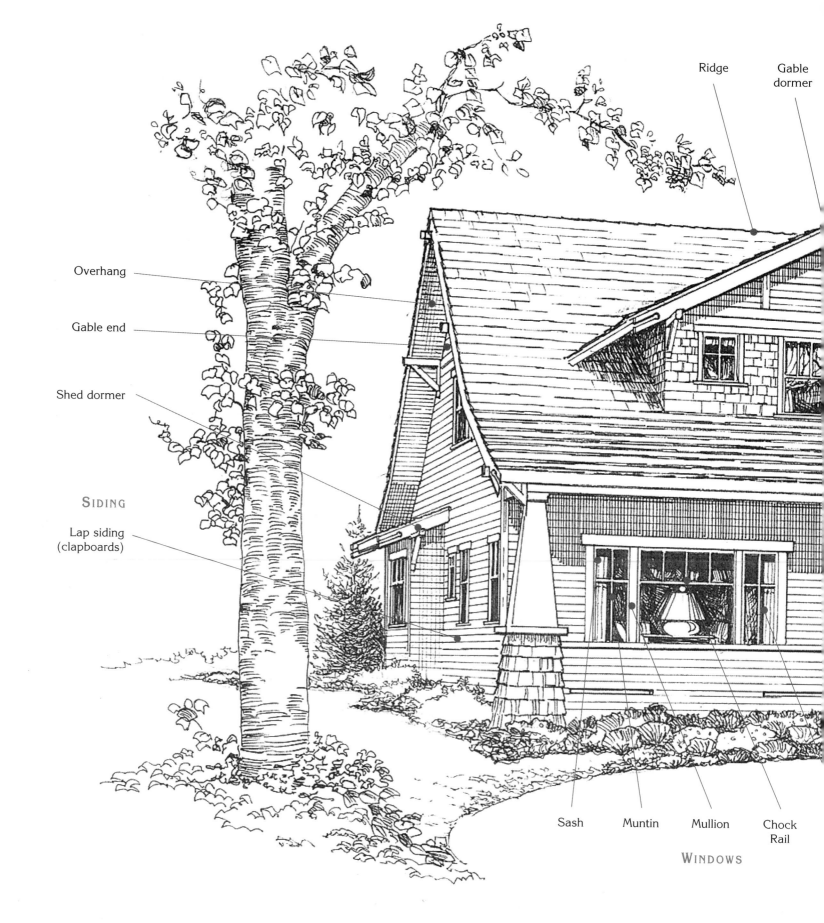

Ridge

Gable
dormer

Overhang

Gable end

Shed dormer

SIDING

Lap siding
(clapboards)

Sash   Muntin   Mullion   Chock
Rail

WINDOWS

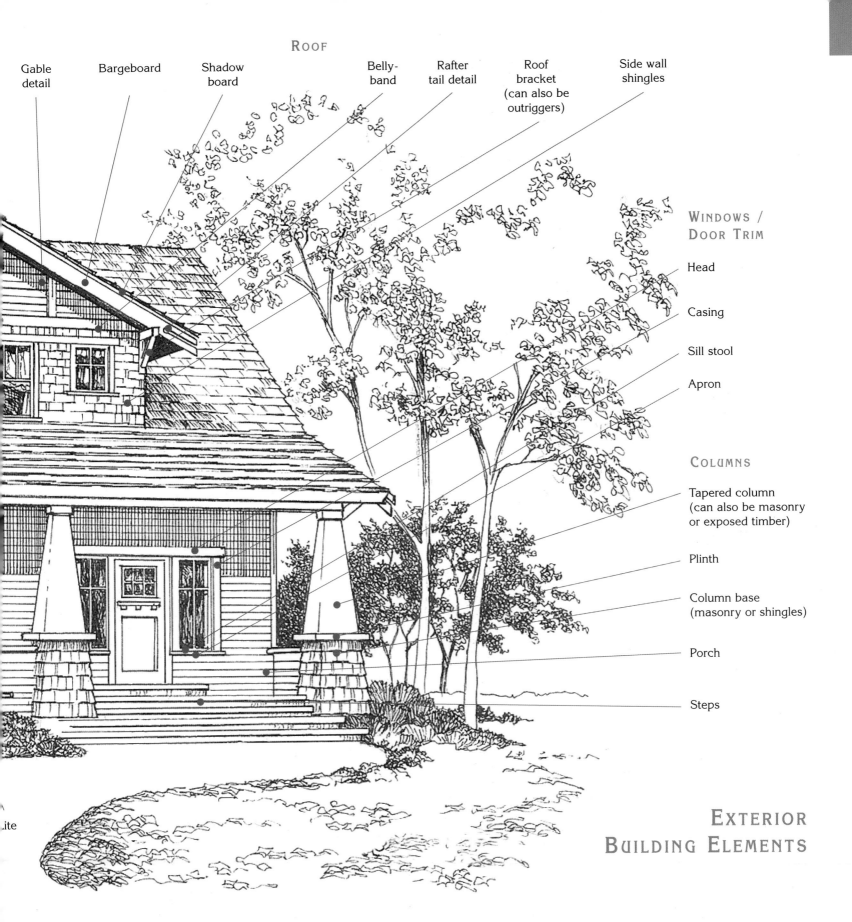

ROOF

Gable detail

Bargeboard

Shadow board

Belly-band

Rafter tail detail

Roof bracket (can also be outriggers)

Side wall shingles

WINDOWS / DOOR TRIM

Head

Casing

Sill stool

Apron

COLUMNS

Tapered column (can also be masonry or exposed timber)

Plinth

Column base (masonry or shingles)

Porch

Steps

...ite

EXTERIOR BUILDING ELEMENTS

THE NEW TRADITIONAL BUNGALOW:

FAMILY HOMES FOR THE NEW MILLENNIUM

: STEEPED IN HISTORY, the new traditional bungalow encompasses many characteristics synonymous with the original bungalows of the early part of the 1900s. Large front porches, generous roof overhangs, intricately detailed roof brackets, and sweeping second-floor dormers are a few elements that define the architectural vocabulary indigenous to the bungalow style. Craftsmanship, attention to detail, and freedom to express new and regional architectural details create an evolutionary architecture that gracefully evolves with a continually changing culture. However familiar, the bungalow form has been redefined to reflect the lifestyles of a new generation of families reinforcing the Arts & Crafts bungalow as an icon in American culture and an architectural style reflective of people and time. The bungalows in this section have been chosen for their sympathetic reinterpretation of the architectural elements that define the bungalow.

The bungalow plans that follow illustrate how designers, architects, and builders have created new prototypes that are traditionally inspired yet have evolved to work within the framework of current planning concepts and housing needs.

■ ■

THE TUMALO

Size: 2,309 sq. ft.
Main floor: 1,262 sq. ft.
Upper floor: 1,047 sq. ft.
Detached garage: 576 sq. ft.
Garage studio: 300 sq. ft.
Designer: The Bungalow Company
Builder: Spellman Construction

: THE GOAL WAS TO DEVELOP a Greene & Greene–inspired bungalow home on a large in-town building lot. Difficulty was encountered after discovering that a large portion of the lot was off-limits to building due to wetlands setbacks and the requirement for an on-site septic system. The possibility of building this type of bungalow seemed to all but disappear after several attempts to spread the plan out within the required setbacks. After revisiting the site, the designer regrouped and concentrated on condensing the floor plan, still intent on capturing the esthetic of the original Greene & Greene homes. The designer focused on the use of exposed timber and the reinterpretation of original details to draw the Greene & Greene influence into the project. The home location in Puget Sound receives substantially more precipitation than southern California, presented a challenge of how to translate the details and style to an inclement climate and

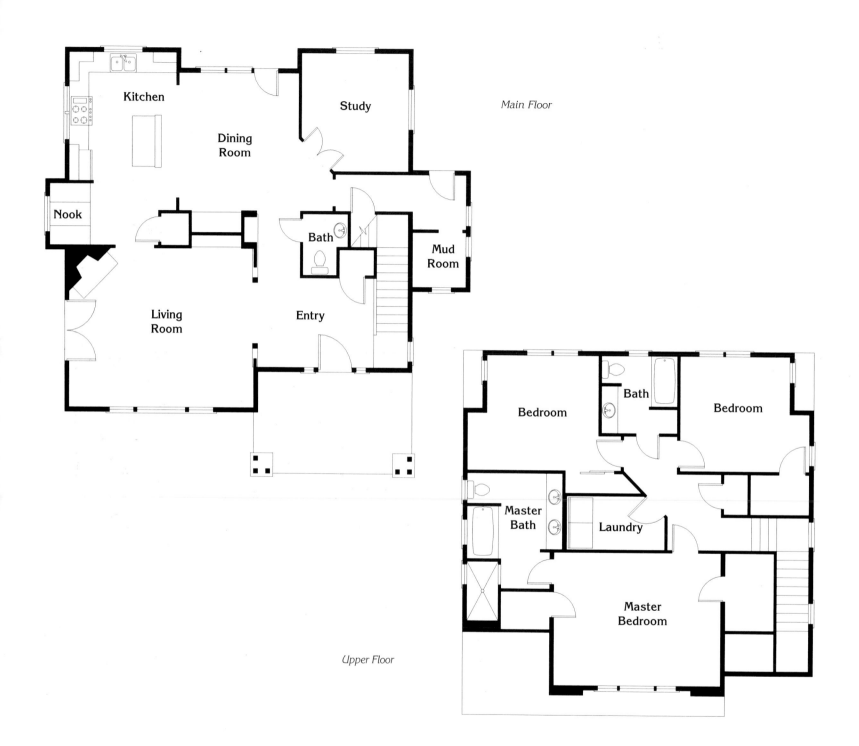

Kitchen

Dining Room

Study

Main Floor

Nook

Bath

Mud Room

Living Room

Entry

Bedroom

Bath

Bedroom

Master Bath

Laundry

Master Bedroom

Upper Floor

develop a home that would stand the test of time. The main floor plan focused on bringing light into all rooms from several directions and creating connections to adjacent rooms with arched doorways. These features make the modest floor plan feel much larger and, in the spirit of the Greenes, connect the architecture to nature.

The second-floor living space is located primarily within the roof structure, providing ample opportunity to experience the nooks and crannies created in a story-and-a-half home. The warm interior color palette and cherry cabinetry create an environment that brightens the most overcast Washington days. Craftsmen and general contractors David and Irving Spellman adorned the living room with beamed ceilings and arched doorways between rooms, which softens the transition between rooms and creates a comforting flow to the home. Inspired by the original Greene & Greene masterworks, this home illustrates how the bungalow style can be translated into different scales for any geographical region.

THE HODGES MANZANITA

Size: 2,576 sq. ft.
Main floor: 1,552 sq. ft.
Upper floor: 1,024 sq. ft.
Designer: The Bungalow Company
Builder: Spellman Construction

THE ERICKSON MANZANITA

Size: 2,604 sq. ft.
Main floor: 1,388 sq. ft.
Upper floor: 1,216 sq. ft.
Designer: The Bungalow Company
Builder: Spellman Construction

: INSPIRED BY A TRADITIONAL BUNGALOW designed by Frederick Ackerman in the early part of the last century, the Manzanita plan was designed to work in urban-infill building lots and new, traditionally planned neighborhoods. The Manzanita, like the Ackerman plan of the 1920s, was designed as a stock plan, with the intent of the design being easily reproduced in different locations with varied exterior looks. Simply changing the window massing, eave detailing, or columns can create a substantially different look for the home.

The Manzanita porch is detailed with exposed timber columns and beams that are connected with intricately designed wood connectors. The porch creates a comfortable vantage point for the homeowner to observe neighborhood life. Large-scaled brick or stucco

This cook's dream kitchen is open and functional with plenty of work surfaces.

columns give the porch a solid presence, and layered cedar shingles below the porch create a logical hierarchy of materials. The use of natural-cedar shingle siding and painted-cedar lap siding is used to reproduce traditional materials. Latticework in the gable ends emulates a traditional bungalow ventilation detail and provides an opportunity for distinctive detailing.

Both based on the Manzanita stock plan, the main floors of the Hodges and Erickson plans illustrated here have a centrally located kitchen that includes a breakfast nook with peekaboo views to the entry and living room. The dining room is open to the living room and kitchen, while full leaded-glass pocket doors separate it from the study. Painted window casings, baseboard, and ceiling molding highlight the natural-wood windows and doors.

Nestled under the stairs, the breakfast nook is connected to the house by peekaboo openings.

tional work counter. The main floor of the Hodges' home offers a master bedroom while the Erickson home uses the space as a study.

The upper level of the Erickson plan consists of three bedrooms, two bathrooms, and a laundry room, removing the need to transport clothes up and down the stairs. The playroom is conveniently located on the second floor, adjacent to the children's bedrooms and providing easy access to toys and homework materials.

The kitchen sink is centered in front of two large windows that provide ample light and views. Kitchen cabinets line the walls while an island floats in the center, creating an addi-

Either plan can be adapted to accommodate a full basement.

The Hodges Manzanita

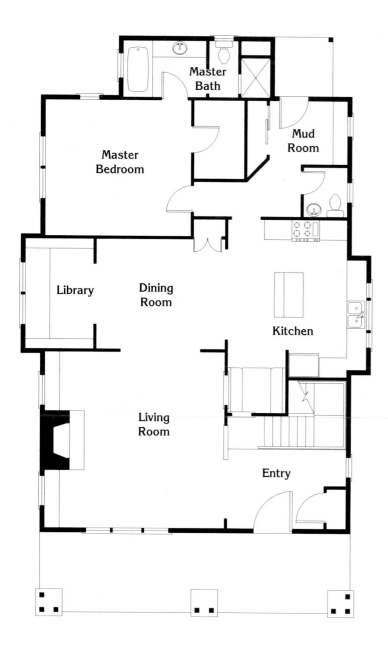

Main Floor

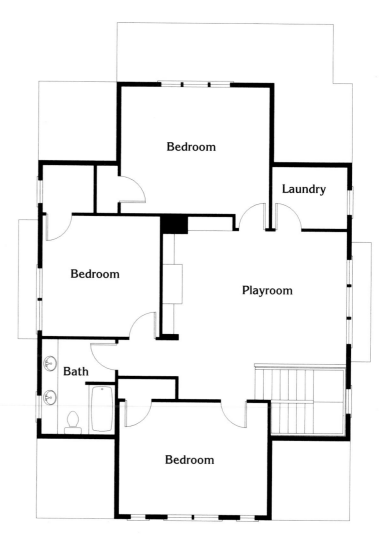

Upper Floor

The Erickson Manzanita

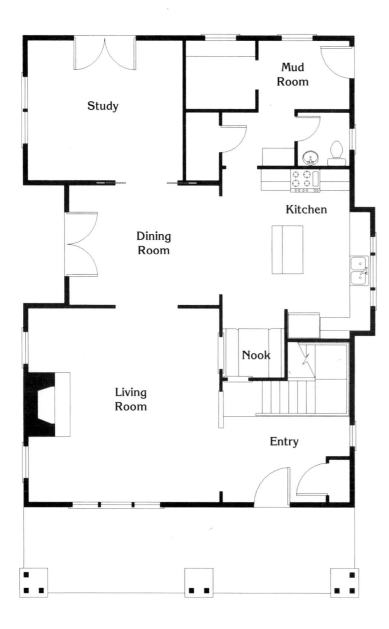

Main Floor

Upper Floor

THE BIRCH

Size: 2,180 sq. ft.
Main floor: 1,140 sq. ft.
Upper floor: 1,040 sq. ft.
Designer: The Bungalow Company
Builder: Reese Construction

: As COMMUNITIES ARE DESIGNED more densely, narrow building lots have become more common. The Birch plan was designed to accommodate narrower lots, with a maximum building width of twenty-eight feet. The garages are detached or can be connected with a breezeway and accessed from either the front or the rear of the home by an alley. The front porch is the full width of the house, creating a flexible outdoor room that is a transition from public to private space. The entry hall houses the stairway to the upper floor and allows light to enter from a leaded-glass window next to the stair landing.

Guests and residents circulate through the living room, where two higher windows create an ideal space for furniture or built-in cabinets. The high windows allow for light to enter while

Traditionally a sideboard, this wine cabinet/chef's desk incorporates modern function into traditional architectural elements of the bungalow.

flow in from both directions. The den is connected to the dining room with a pair of French doors and allows access to the home from the backyard. Adjacent to the kitchen is a mud room, which connects to the garage and includes a powder room and mechanical room.

Builders Trisha and Jerry Reese have detailed the home with five-panel clear fir doors and custom fir cabinetry, bringing timeless warmth to the home. The upper floor consists of two bedrooms at the rear of the house that share a large bathroom. The master bedroom is in the front of the home and contains the ultimate master bath with a walk-in shower, soaking tub, compartmentalized toilet, and double vanity. The walk-in closet has two windows that allow in light and fresh air. The laundry room is located on the second floor to eliminate hauling laundry up and down the stairs.

still maintaining a sense of privacy. The separation of dining and living rooms is achieved with a pair of square columns and quarter-height walls. The cased opening between the dining room and living room maintains the rooms' identities while still keeping an open floor plan. The kitchen and dining room are connected and work in tandem, creating a room that is the full width of the house and allowing light to

A front-facing gable roof is clad in cedar shingles and is highlighted by symmetrically placed upper-story windows. The three front-porch columns frame the living room windows and single front door; the gable roof over the front door clearly identifies the entry. The main-floor siding is cedar lap siding, which extends up to the upper-floor line. Continuous shed dormers run on each side of the home, providing ample interior space for the upper floor. A two-foot projection from the dining room is covered by a shed roof and provides extra interior floor space for the dining room while breaking up the long exterior wall.

Main Floor

Bath

Mud Room

Study

Kitchen

Dining Room

Entry

Living Room

Porch

Upper Floor

Bedroom

Bedroom

Bath

Master Bath

Laundry

Master Bedroom

THE CHERRY

Size: 2,182 sq. ft.
Main floor: 1,320 sq. ft.
Upper floor: 862 sq. ft.
Designer: The Bungalow Company
Builder: Reese Construction

: DESIGNED FOR A DENSELY PLANTED traditional neighborhood, the Cherry plan focuses on creating areas of retreat within the home while connecting the public areas of the home to the neighborhood. The half front porch houses a single column or column timber-cluster and a single front door flanked by sidelights. The entry door frames a Craftsman-detailed newel post and stairway. Opposite the stairway is a cased opening to the living room, which focuses on a corner fireplace. The natural-wood fireplace surround has a dark finish in the tradition of the bungalow style, while the natural-slate front is highlighted by three Arts & Crafts–inspired tiles. The living room windows are flush with the front porch, allowing natural light to flood the living room. The dining room is centrally located and functions as a family gathering place. The kitchen is conveniently

To re-create his childhood bungalow memories, this homeowner collaborated with Reese Construction on this elegant angled Craftsman fireplace. Steve Harrison design.

of the house creates a mud room, which allows for a powder room and coat closet and provides connection to the detached garage. A large master bedroom entered off the angled hallway contains a walk-in closet and generous bathroom with soaking tub. Three well-proportioned second-floor bedrooms are accessed from the front-entry stair and share a compartmentalized bathroom, which allows for multiple family members to prepare for the day simultaneously. A large laundry room is located on the second floor, with ample room to fold laundry or to iron. A bank of three high windows, located above the washer and dryer, lights the work area. Shed and gabled front dormers nestle

located off the dining room and is built of clear vertical grain fir, which provides a rich visual backdrop to the dining room.

Located to the right of the dining room is a den, separated by French doors that provide privacy for work or study. An angled hallway leading to the rear

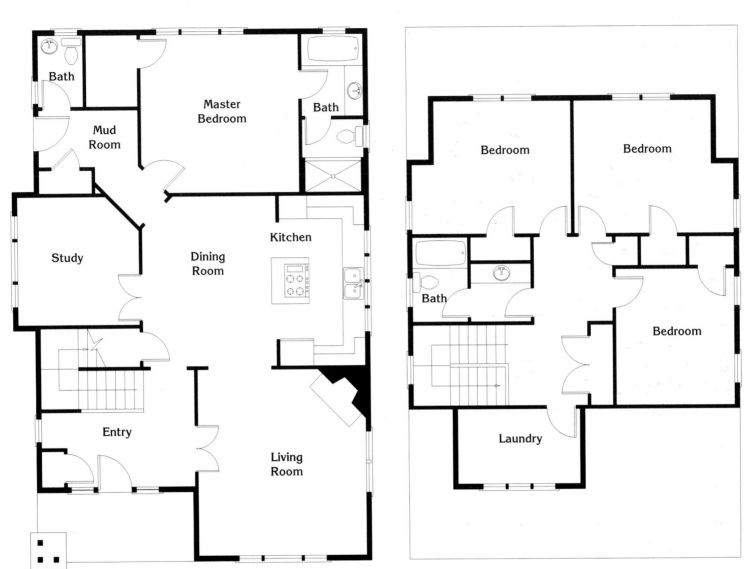

Main Floor

Upper Floor

the home into the neighborhood and create a familiar bungalow form. Gable details of diamond-shaped gridwork are painted khaki green and framed by fresh white bargeboards and belly-bands, while the warm yellow body of the home contrasts with the surrounding green landscape.

HOUSE ON THE HILL

Size: 1,858 sq. ft.
Main floor: 978 sq. ft.
Upper floor: 880 sq. ft.
Attached garage: 528 sq. ft.
Designer: Cottage Designs
Builder: Howcroft Construction

: FINDING OPPORTUNITY IN A STEEP, rocky building lot, owners Ben and Lisa Husaby and designer Al Tozer Jr. developed a landmark home.

Combining traditional bungalow design elements with an eclectic mix of contemporary materials and oversized glazing, the Husaby residence captures sunlight and dramatic city views from its rocky perch.

In response to city height limits, the design required a low-pitched roofline. To balance the vertical orientation of the home and shelter the occupants from the high desert summer sun, generous overhangs and substantial barge rafters were used in conjunction with unique hand-scribed brackets to highlight the roof's importance.

With a total of four levels cascading over a rocky basalt ledge, the Husabys' home embraces the site and honors the existing topography. The owners' favorite space is a wine cellar located under the house alongside huge volcanic boulders.

Two levels of wide-view porches characterize the front elevation, while the garage is located at the rear of the home so as to de-emphasize the role of the automobile.

Interior space is highlighted by an open, light-filled, main-level "great room" that, in combination with the large picture windows, extends perceived space far beyond the home's modest 1,800 square feet.

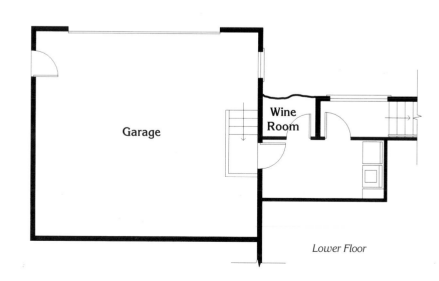

Garage

Wine Room

Lower Floor

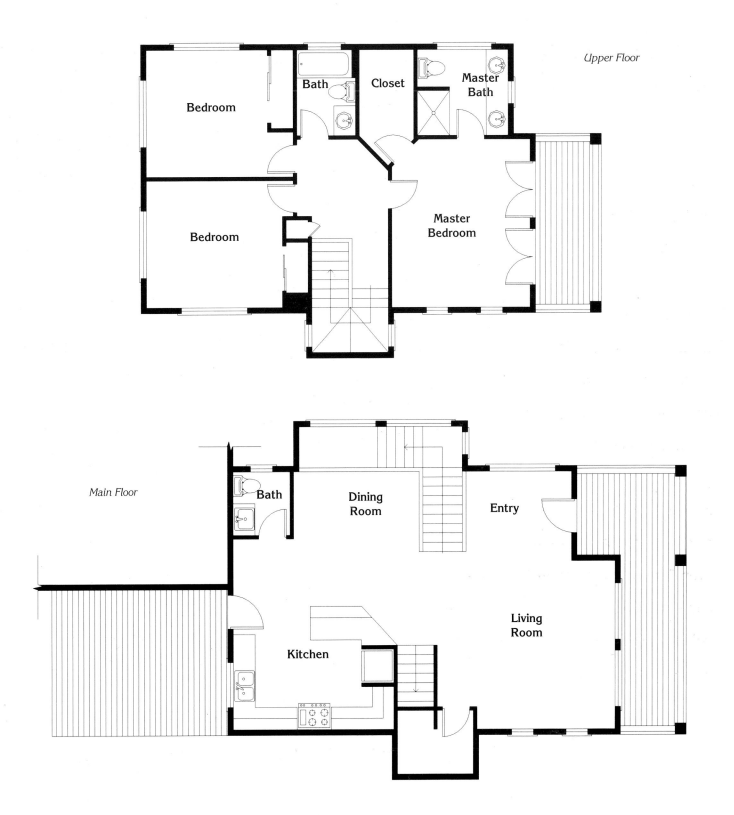

Upper Floor

Bedroom

Bath

Closet

Master
Bath

Bedroom

Master
Bedroom

Main Floor

Bath

Dining
Room

Entry

Living
Room

Kitchen

PLAN BOOK ARCHITECTURE/ STOCK PLANS

■ ■

Like the original bungalow movement, which created abundant neighborhoods and housing prototypes that shaped the urban fabric of this country, today's plan-book architecture provides homebuyers with similar design solutions. However, as many of the planning principles of the early part of this century are reworked in an effort to reinvent our most treasured communities, many of the home plans and concepts of the last two decades have become obsolete.

Purchasing stock plans is often an economical approach when planning to build a new home, but it is imperative that the consumer understands that some modifications to structural, environmental, building code, and mechanical systems may be needed to adapt a specific design.

Structural modifications are the most common required changes made to stock plans; every region of the country has different design requirements based on the local climate conditions and in which seismic zone the home is to be located. Prior to purchasing a stock plan, the consumer should verify the following information with the plan company or home designer:

: What snow load was the plan designed for?

: What wind speed was the plan designed for?

: Which seismic zone was the plan designed for?

: What building code and edition was the plan designed for?

: Has this home plan ever been constructed?

The consumer should verify with their building official that the plan design criteria could work in that region. If it does not, a local designer, engineer, or architect will need to modify the plans. It is always recommended that a design professional review plans for a specific site, and coordinate the structural, heating, cooling, and ventilation systems for the home.

Properly locating a new home on a building site usually requires the help of a seasoned professional. Before purchasing a home plan, create a preliminary site plan by identifying property line dimensions, property easements, topography, and the location of all utilities. If the site is undeveloped land, the well and on-site septic location must be identified on the plan. Once the preliminary site plan is drawn, your local building or planning department can help you identify the building setbacks and any other regulations that may dictate how the property is developed and the house sited. Often homes that are being built in planned communities or subdivisions will be required to undergo an architectural review prior to submitting for a building permit. A study set of drawings can usually be purchased from a designer or plan company prior to committing to a full set of construction documents. This drawing set can help identify the actual length, width, and height of the building and aid in determining if the house will fit on the property. The study set typically costs between $50 and $200 and should include exterior elevation, which your design professional can use to illustrate how the home will fit on the site. The set can also be used to establish a preliminary budget; however, complete drawings and specifications will be required to finalize a price. Construction drawings should not be purchased for the home until it has been identified that the building fits the site and a preliminary budget has been established.

Prices for stock plans vary from $300 to $1,500, depending upon the complexity of the design and the pricing structure of the designer or plan company. If you develop a custom plan with a designer or architect you should be prepared to pay 5 to 10 percent of the construction cost. For an hourly rate, local design professionals can review plans to ensure compliance with local building codes. For a percentage of the contract, design professionals can also be hired to manage the construction contract between you and your builder. The best money and time spent is that spent researching your builder and retaining one with good references from clients, suppliers, lending institutions, and other design and building professionals. Building a new home is never free of additional decisions and clarifications, so you need to hire a builder who is reliable, trustworthy, and a good communicator.

When budgeting for a new home, design fees can sometimes appear to be a luxury; but to build a new home that is on budget, on time, and without disappointment, it is imperative that you and your builder are clear on the plans and specifications of the home. The work and money required to develop a clear set of plans and specifications is outweighed by the efficiency and professionalism with which your project will be executed. Building officials, suppliers, subcontractors, and lending institutions all need information from the plans, and the clearer the information the fewer questions and delays will occur. Suppliers and subcontractors develop bids and pricing from the plans and specifications, so the more complete the work the more accurate your budget will be. Despite popular belief, most home builders operate on a modest profit margin, so the reality of a builder covering some large unforeseen discrepancy or omission in estimating due to inaccurate or lack of information on the plans and specifications is highly unlikely. Detailed up-front planning will make for a less stressful building process and ensure that in the end your home is everything you desired.

■ ■

THE TAMARACK

Size: 1,988 sq. ft.
Main floor: 1,988 sq. ft.
Attached garage: 735 sq. ft.
Designer: Cottage Designs
Builder: Howcroft Construction

BARREL-VAULTED PORCH CEILINGS and an arched, full-divided-light entry door warmly welcome guests to the Tamarack. Capitalizing on a rear sloping lot, the Tamarack provides single-level living with an oversized two-car garage tucked underneath.

Tamarack's two barrel-vaulted porch ceilings, three exterior-view decks, and generous contemporary use of large window areas dominate the unique exterior elevations. The large glazed windows allow for awe-inspiring views and collect the early morning sun's rays.

Designed with the concept of "the hearth is the home," the Tamarack has a centrally located kitchen that is visually connected to the dining and living areas while maintaining panoramic views beyond. A slight change in floor height and flooring materials defines the open light-filled living room.

The efficient "mail room" and office is located close to the stairway and is adjacent to the dining area. Ideal for paying bills and accessing the Internet, this functional niche is a welcome alternative to the standard overflowing kitchen counter.

Lower Floor

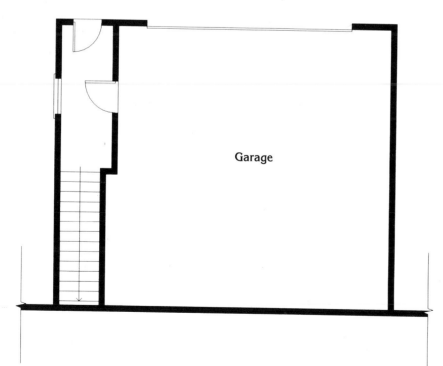

Garage

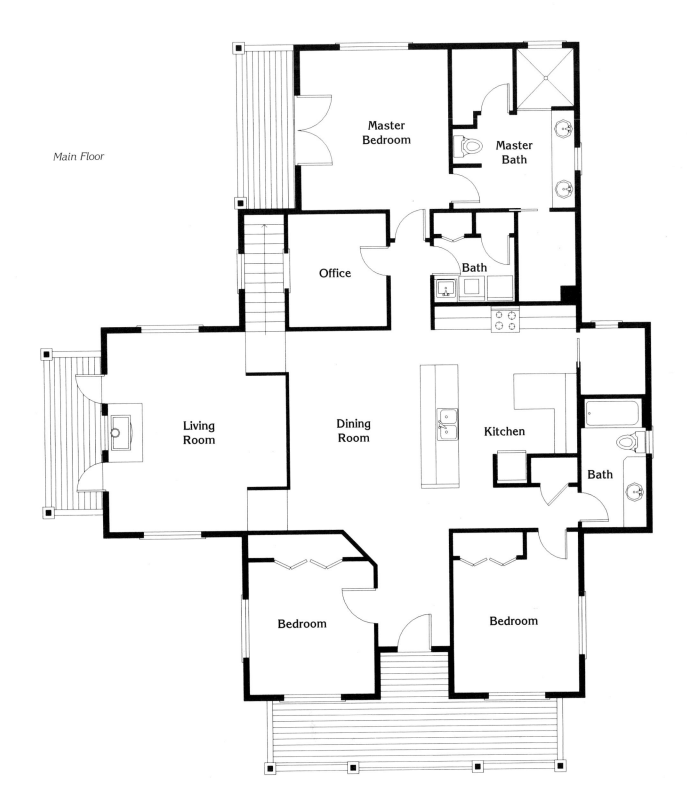

Main Floor

Master Bedroom

Master Bath

Office

Bath

Living Room

Dining Room

Kitchen

Bath

Bedroom

Bedroom

MIDDEN POINT—
THE WENZLAU RESIDENCE

Size: 2,400 sq. ft.
Main floor: 1,200 sq. ft.
Upper floor: 900 sq. ft.
Studio (over garage): 300 sq. ft.
Designer: Wenzlau Architects
Builder: Tom White

: THE WENZLAU IS A COMPACT HOME that draws upon the traditions of the bungalow home without attempting to replicate one. After searching in vain for an older home that hadn't been tampered with, the Wenzlaus settled on building a new home. The setting for the home is in a new neighborhood within walking distance of town. The lot they selected was narrow in width and bounded by mature trees. In large part, the site determined how the layout of the home would be approached.

The goal was to create a home that looked as though it could have been there for many years. After several attempts at various layouts, a simple plan was arrived at that satisfied the goal for a compact house with lots of natural light. The design concept groups all of the rooms around a central stair hall that brings light into the center of the house, which is ideal for the home's Northwest location. The central stair location also eliminates the need for hallways and provides a focus to the whole house. The main floor has no doors between rooms, allowing each room to flow into the next while maintaining the desired separations between each activity—a common characteristic of traditional bungalows. The house, which is zoned from front to back, changes from a quieter living area to the kitchen/eating area, which functions as the hub for daily activities. The dining room with wraparound windows is a flexible space used for a variety of family projects. The overall plan was carefully composed to create symmetry and balance, yet maintains an informal appearance throughout with its varying rooflines and window placements.

Instead of the traditional two-car garage, the Wenzlaus built a porte cochere, which offers shelter from the rain and provides a visual connection to the garden at the rear. The garage forms an L-shaped entry court that leads to the covered entry. The garage houses a studio with its own entry, which could serve as a future in-law unit. The home sits in harmony on the lot and successfully blends modern needs with past traditions, creating a comfortable home.

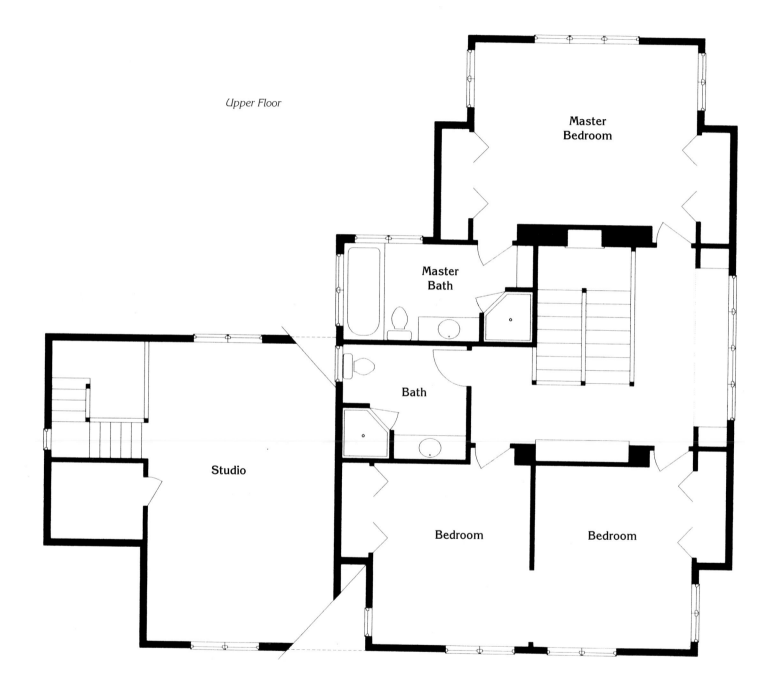

Upper Floor

Master
Bedroom

Master
Bath

Bath

Studio

Bedroom

Bedroom

Main Floor

Living Room

Entry

Dining Room

Bath

Garage

Kitchen

Utility Room

The New England Craftsman

Size: 3,792 sq. ft.
Main floor: 1,380 sq. ft.
Upper floor: 1,032 sq. ft.
Daylight basement: 1,380 sq. ft.
Designer/Builder: Eric Lewtas/Architect

: Building their own home had always been a dream for architect Eric Lewtas and his wife Winnie Skeates. Since maintaining a budget was a key component to building their own home, Lewtas took care in developing an efficient design that worked for their lifestyle.

Planned with extreme New Hampshire winters in mind, the entry transitions from a covered front porch to an enclosed mud room with lots of storage for heavy winter clothing. The kitchen is located in the upper right-hand corner of the home and overlooks the dayroom and entry. Adjacent to the kitchen, a screened-in porch provides sanctuary on hot summer evenings and connects the house with the environment by extending living to the outdoors. The dayroom doubles as a dining room and features an eastern-facing bay window to capture morning sun. To achieve a high level of finish, interior details were designed to be simple and straightforward while utilizing local available materials. The home office is accessed from the front entry and along the main circulation hall that connects the living room to the kitchen, entry, and dayroom. Half walls separate the home office from the living room, creating an open living area while developing adequate areas for work and furniture placement. The step down to the living room signals arrival in a special place, while the northern-facing bay window creates an ideal reading nook. The living room spans the entire width of the home, allowing light to enter the room from three sides. An open, half-turn staircase connects the main floor with the daylight basement and the second floor. Two bedrooms and a bathroom share the east end of the home, while the west end houses a walk-in closet, large master bedroom, and bath. The north and south bedroom walls are five feet tall revealing the roofline of the building, which creates a cozy nest under the eaves.

Steeped in detail and quality, this New Hampshire bungalow combines Yankee ingenuity with the Arts & Crafts tradition to create a bungalow that will stand not only the cold New Hampshire winters but also the test of time.

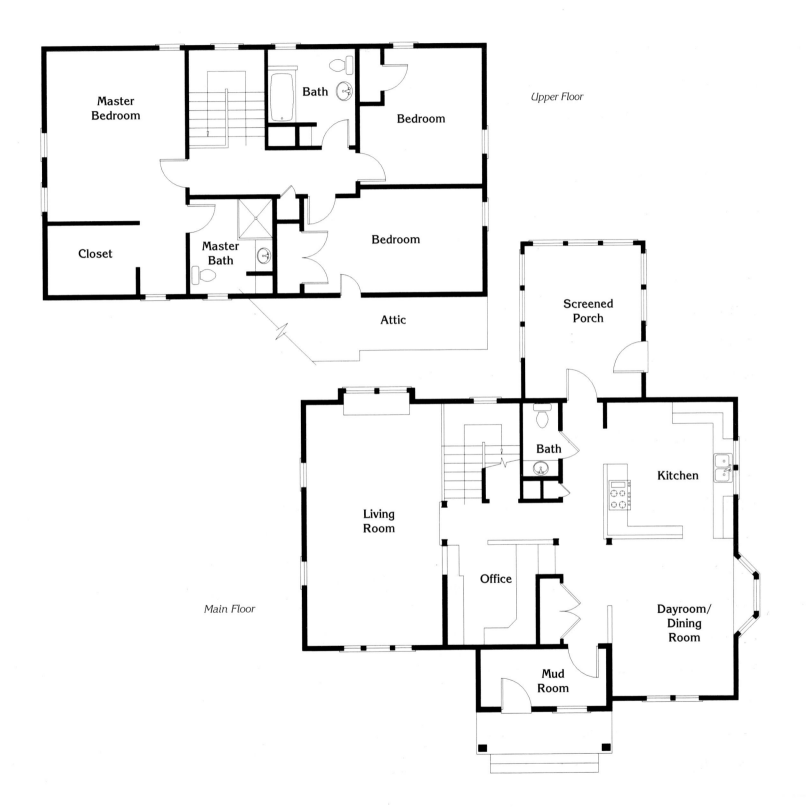

Master
Bedroom

Bath

Upper Floor

Bedroom

Closet

Master
Bath

Bedroom

Attic

Screened
Porch

Bath

Kitchen

Living
Room

Main Floor

Office

Dayroom/
Dining
Room

Mud
Room

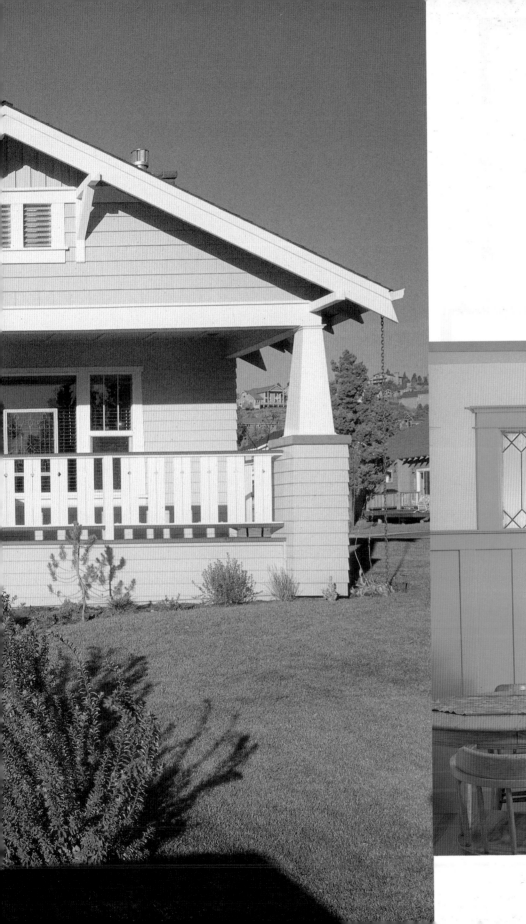

THE GREY HAWK
Size: 1,838 sq. ft.
Main floor: 1,838 sq. ft.
Attached garage: 528 sq. ft.
Designer: Tom Tanner
Builder: Tanner Construction

The fireplace is located at the heart of the bungalow.

: NESTLED IN A NEW and traditionally planned neighborhood, the Grey Hawk plan has an attached garage served by an authentically scaled alley. Builder and designer Tom Tanner set out to develop a flexible plan that could be built numerous times in a single neighborhood without creating a redundant architectural form. For this plan to be effective, it was imperative that the design was easy to modify and simple to build. The use of premanufactured roof trusses on this single-story home allows for distinctive roof forms to appear on each version of this home. Bungalow porches were custom-designed for each rendition of this home and tailored specifically to address each site's features. In the true nature of the bungalow, exterior colors for this home were chosen to be simple and understated, creating a timeless reinterpretation of the neighborhood bungalows that filled America's neighborhoods a century ago. The use of medium-density fiberboard and trim stock throughout the house provides an economical method for creating authentically detailed, paint-grade woodwork. In the bungalow tradition, the dining room is paneled with a panel-and-batten wainscot. High windows make good use of space, allowing for the placement of high or oversized furniture. The gas-burning fireplace, flanked by tall windows, creates the heart of this bungalow, and the mirror above the fireplace as well as the vaulted ceiling create a more spacious feel within this traditional bungalow form.

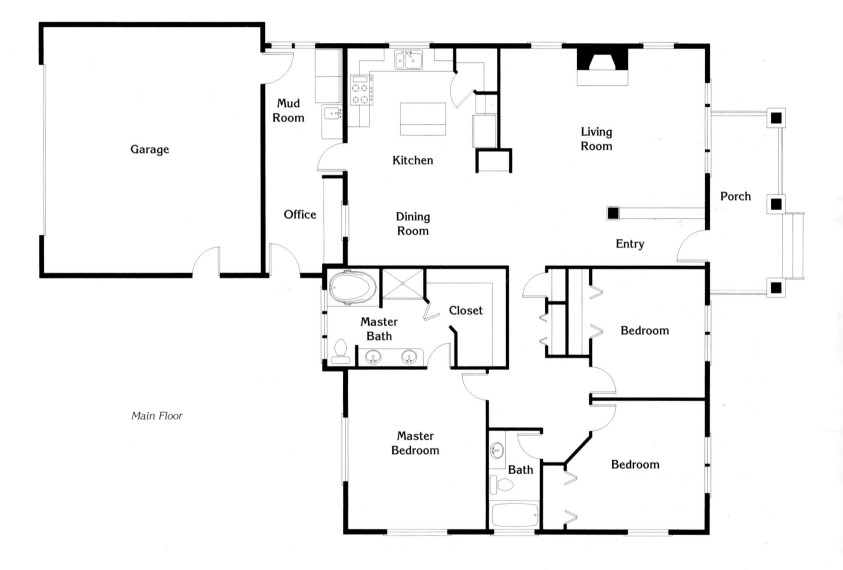

Garage

Mud Room

Office

Kitchen

Dining Room

Living Room

Porch

Entry

Master Bath

Closet

Bedroom

Master Bedroom

Bath

Bedroom

Main Floor

The Wilshire

Size: 2,496 sq. ft.
Main floor: 1,856 sq. ft.
Second floor: 640 sq. ft.
Designer: Ashmore/Kessenich Design

: THE CLIENT KNEW HE WANTED to build a bungalow and, better than that, he understood that the heart and soul of a bungalow lies in the details. Through their collaboration, designer and client created a home that met the client's needs and was at home on the high arid farmland in Eastern Washington. The front façade is symmetrically designed and is shaded from the elements by a full-width front porch; a single shed dormer set into the gently curved roof balances the front elevation. A porte cochere leading to the side entry provides direct access to the kitchen. Materials such as stucco siding and tapered brick columns were chosen for the extreme Washington climate, while exposed timber work accents the gable ends.

Like a classic bungalow, the foyer opens through a cased doorway to the

This traditional Arts & Crafts fireplace is centered on a boxed beam ceiling.

a built-in hutch, and a window seat. The kitchen is highlighted by fir cabinetry and is accented with a subway-tile backsplash. The kitchen overlooks an enclosed sunroom with exercise pool and French doors that provide access to the backyard. Located in the left rear corner of the home is the master suite, which includes a compartmentalized bathroom and walk-in closet. Hexagonal one-inch floor tiles and subway-tile wainscot reproduce the sense of quality and attention to detail that make the bungalow famous. The second floor includes two additional bedrooms and a bath that are accessed by a centrally located stairway.

living room on the right and through a pair of pocket doors to a study on the left. A colonnade connects the living room to the dining room, with authentically proportioned beamed ceilings,

Main Floor

Upper Floor

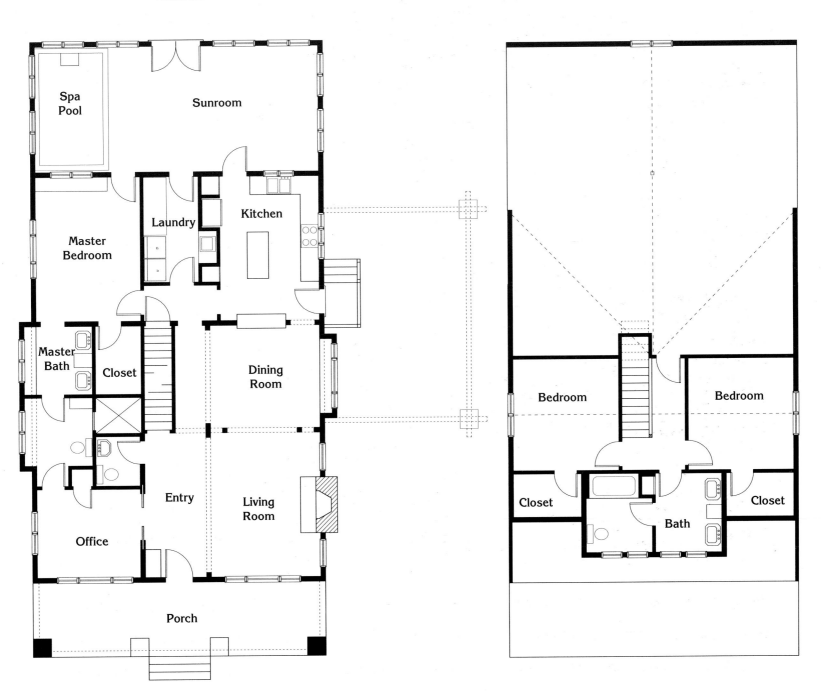

Spa Pool

Sunroom

Kitchen

Laundry

Master Bedroom

Master Bath

Closet

Dining Room

Entry

Living Room

Office

Porch

Bedroom

Bedroom

Closet

Closet

Bath

The Plinth

Size: 1,978 sq. ft.
First floor: 988 sq. ft.
Second floor: 990 sq. ft.
Attached garage: 528 sq. ft.
Designer: Scott Gilbride/Architect
Contractor: Howcroft Construction

: THIS BUNGALOW-STYLE HOME was designed to be built as two different homes on two adjacent lots with a sloped terrain towards the street. The challenge was to utilize the same conceptual plan for both lots while creating unique qualities for each home. By providing subtle variations to the exterior elevations and detailing unique color choices, revising the front porch stairway entrances, and flipping the overall floor plan, the designer was able to create enough diversity of materials, forms, and textures to produce a different solution for each lot. These variations were continued on the interiors, where different choices for the finish materials—such as tile, hardwoods, trims, and detailing—allowed each homeowner to maintain his own individuality.

This house uses the same floor plan but is given a different look by modifying the exterior elevation.

Conceptually, the plan takes best advantage of the vista of the neighboring foothills seen from the main room—living, dining, and kitchen; the covered front porch; and the master bedroom upstairs. As is traditional with bungalows, one enters into the main public spaces first where many built-in cabinets have been incorporated. However, the plan reflects modern sensibilities such as a minimum of dividing walls between rooms, the openness of the first-floor plan, and the transfer of light from room to room.

The upstairs is a more traditional bungalow layout, with charming attic-like spaces created by the roof structure. These areas have been carefully crafted to use every possible space effectively and to provide ample storage and sleeping quarters.

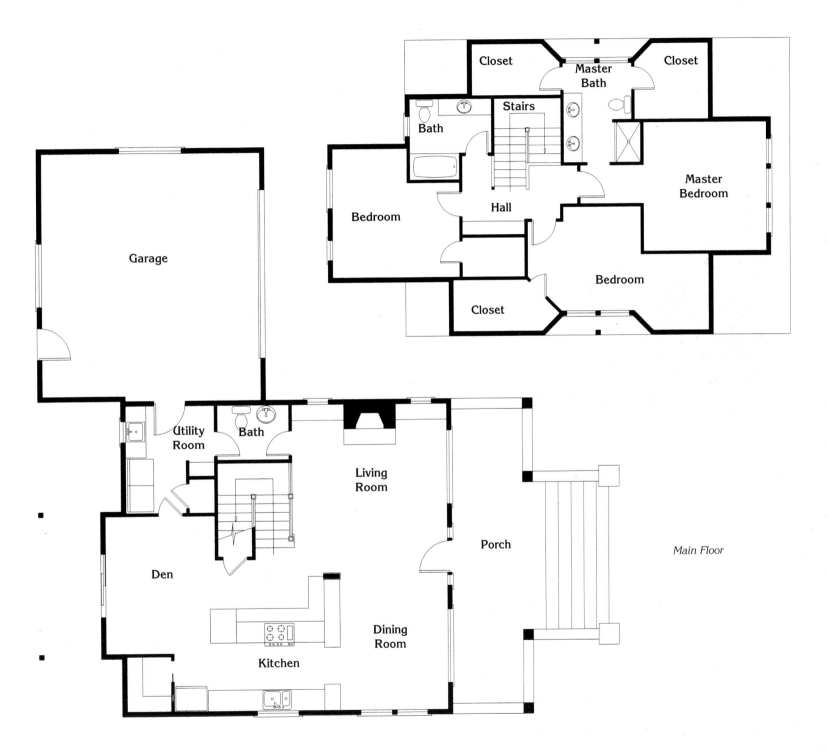

Upper Floor

Closet

Master
Bath

Closet

Bath

Stairs

Master
Bedroom

Bedroom

Hall

Bedroom

Closet

Garage

Utility
Room

Bath

Living
Room

Porch

Main Floor

Den

Dining
Room

Kitchen

THE WINSLOW

Size: 2,560 sq. ft.
Main floor: 1,403 sq. ft.
Attached garage: 1,157 sq. ft.
Designer: The Bungalow Company
Contractor: Spellman Construction

: PERCHED ABOVE THE STREET in a new bungalow neighborhood developed by Spellman Construction, The Winslow embodies all of the elements that define a classic American bungalow. An asymmetrically placed gable dormer creates visual interest within the large roof form and is balanced by the gabled entry to the front porch. The porch sweeps across the entire front of the house, creating a comfortable refuge for hot summer or rainy winter days. Sage-green cedar-lap siding and earth-toned cedar shingles blend with the evergreen backdrop and are highlighted by crisp white bargeboards and trim. The open entry enters directly to the dining room and kitchen area, which take full advantage of the morning sunlight. Craftsmen and general contractors David and Irving Spellman embellished the dining room wainscot and kitchen cabinets by using white-painted bead board. Vertical-grain white-oak flooring throughout the main floor lets each room flow into the next; a cased opening defines the entry from the dining room to the living room and centrally located U-shaped staircase that accesses the two upstairs bedrooms, playroom, a shared bathroom, and a full master suite. The tile fireplace with painted trim is located on an outside wall, with bookcases and high awning windows on each side creating an authentic-feeling bungalow living room. A single large window framed by two single-hung windows looks out on the porch, which provides shade from the direct southern sun but allows ample light to fill the room. A large study is entered from the living room through a pair of French pocket doors. The den has a rear porch, which is served by a pair of French doors that lead outside. A shed roof covers the den bay, helping to break up the large gable-wall elevation. The den leads to the utility area that houses a three-quarter bath, double-door pantry, and mud room with coat closet. All rooms are organized around a centrally located staircase, eliminating the need for hallways. This helps to reduce square footage while allowing each room to receive natural light from two or more directions.

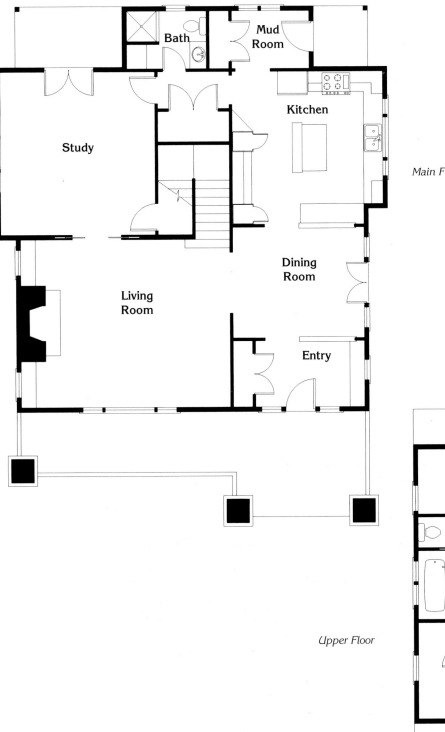

Bath

Mud
Room

Kitchen

Study

Main Floor

Dining
Room

Living
Room

Entry

Laundry

Playroom

Bedroom

Master
Bath

Bath

Upper Floor

Master
Bedroom

Bedroom

COTTAGE BUNGALOWS & GARLOWS:
SMALL LIVES BIG

Bobbitt studio/garlow on its hillside perch.

: AS NEW NEIGHBORHOODS are designed in the spirit of historical communities, designers are forced to deal with a new set of design criteria. In an effort to eliminate urban sprawl and reduce the amount of commuting done by Americans, current planning trends suggest that we create communities that are adjacent to mass transit, or that simply require less commuting. Creating dense urban areas allows planners to maintain undeveloped land for environmental and recreation pursuits while preserving the resources and the environment by reducing fossil fuel consumption.

In creating densely planned communities, designers, planners, and homebuyers are forced to reevaluate their housing needs. Telecommuting has evolved, with the computer and Internet providing alternatives to everyday commuting. The Internet has also reinvented the cottage industries of the last century and made the world everyone's marketplace. To satisfy current technology and transportation needs we are all having to reevaluate how and where we work. Simply adapting an unused bedroom as an at-home office certainly fits the bill for some workers; however, household pressures, privacy, and professionalism are a few of the issues that can wear on the most dedicated worker. New workplaces are being created in homes across America, whether they are an attached home office, an office over a garage, or a detached stand-alone building. Many new homes are being built with structured network wiring that provides flexibility to the telecommuter or entrepreneur who requires information and equipment use from multiple locations. Many other opportunities exist for accessory dwelling units/mother-in-law apartments in denser planned communities. The American dream of three bedrooms and two and one-half baths is evolving as demographics illustrate that people are staying single longer, living longer, and living less traditional lifestyles. As a result, there is a growing need for "unconventional housing types." The stereotypes of apartments being used mostly for single living have changed; buyers and renters are focused on more long-term living solutions that reflect their lifestyle. In addition to the new home office, cottages and garlows are providing alternative living solutions for all demographics, developing communities that reflect varying economic levels and lifestyles.

This garlow was built to blend with its surroundings.

Facing: This garlow's natural wood ceiling and cabinetry bring warmth into the space.

BEND BUNGALOW

Size: 1,624 sq. ft.
Main floor: 1,624 sq. ft.
Attached garage: 576 sq. ft.
Designer: Cottage Designs
Builder: Ironwood Construction

: SNUGGLED UNDER A LOW-PITCHED ROOF, the Bend Bungalow hugs the ground with a comforting and familiar aesthetic of days gone by. Hand-shaped rafter tails, cedar-shingle siding, and tapered exterior-trim detailing exemplify how the combination of quality materials and craftsmanship can work in harmony. This home's generous front porch with well-proportioned columns is an ideal spot to relax or greet the neighbors.

Traditionally styled and planned, this home captures the essence of the original northwest bungalows.

In the true sprit of the original bungalows, this home places people first and autos second with the use of a side-entry garage, located at the back of the house.

The open floor plan invites a more informal lifestyle and allows natural light to flood into the living, dining, and kitchen areas. Efficiently using fewer than 1,700 total square feet, the building budget on this project allowed for high-end finish materials such as solid wood doors, slate and wood flooring, and true divided-light wood windows. A third bedroom/den, separated from the great room by full divided-light pocket doors, makes an ideal home office, media room, or guest room.

Garage

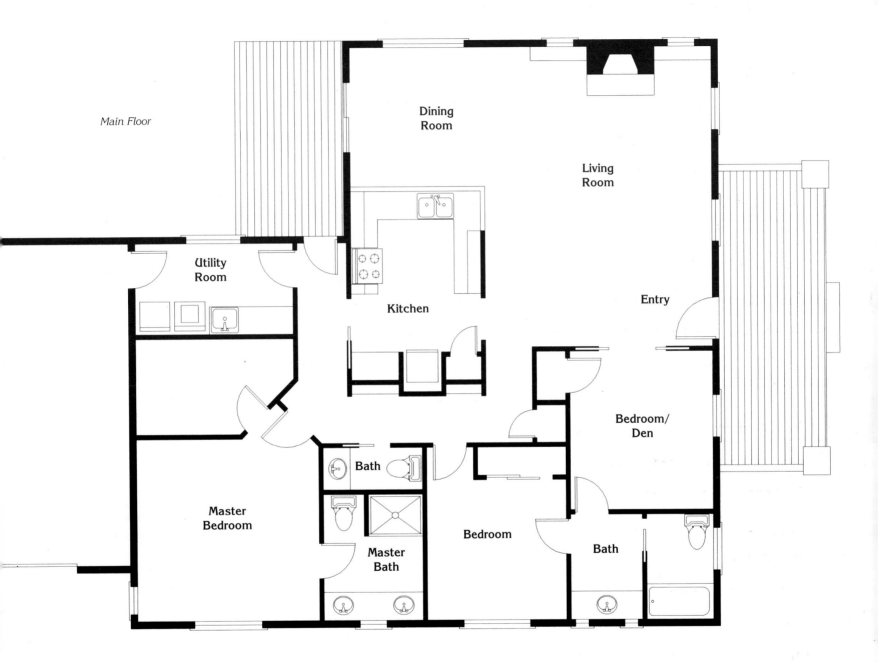

Main Floor

Dining
Room

Living
Room

Utility
Room

Entry

Kitchen

Bedroom/
Den

Bath

Master
Bedroom

Bedroom

Master
Bath

Bath

SCHUBERT RESIDENCE

Size: 1,898 sq. ft.

Main floor: 928 sq. ft.

Upper floor: 970 sq. ft.

Designers: Mike and Debbie Schubert

Builders: Vernon Construction, General Contractor;
   Town & Country Contractors

꞉ MORE THAN JUST A NEW HOUSE, the Schuberts wanted to create a new "old" house in an established neighborhood. Taking cues from the surrounding neighborhood bungalows and a 1920s catalog of house plans, the Schuberts collaborated with a local draftsman and builder team to develop a home that embodied the modest values of the original production bungalows. The historically inspired home yields a modern open floor plan. The main floor focuses on a great room that unites the kitchen, dining, and living areas. The fireplace and entertainment center serve as focal points for the great room, reinforcing the intrinsic family values associated with the bungalow. The study is separated by a half flight of stairs, providing adequate privacy for contemplation or for a visiting guest. The second floor holds two bedrooms, one bath, and a full master suite.

Character-grade maple floors, cherry cabinets, tile countertops, and historically inspired window- and door-trim details illustrate how to sympathetically transition the bungalow into the future with the use of market-ready materials. The use of reproduction lighting and authentically styled exterior doors connect the bungalow's past to the future.

Study

Kitchen

Laundry

Bath

Main Floor

Dining Room

Living Room

Bedroom

Bath

Bedroom

Master Bath

Master Bedroom

Upper Floor

HOUSE IN THE WOODS

Size: 2,135 sq. ft.
Main floor: 1,023 sq. ft.
Upper floor: 1,112 sq. ft.
Dry storage: 222 sq. ft.
Designer: Robert Moore Architect
Builder: Buckner Interior Finishing

: DESIGNED AND BUILT FOR A FAMILY of three with a home-based business, the clients desired an open floor plan with abundant natural light to counter the site's tall trees and heavy shading. Integrated within a forest of cedar trees and ferns, this bungalow reinterpretation enhances the environment by using natural cedar-shingle siding, Douglas fir windows, and a green standing-seam metal roof that meshes with the tree canopy. Shed roofs, large overhangs, and historically proportioned windows identify the bungalow ancestry, while the contemporary organization of the building creates a large central core with natural light flooding into all rooms. The main floor is largely open except for a private home office; a bridge divides the upper floor, separating the bedrooms from a loft and laundry area. Interior shutters connect the master bedroom to the

Upper floor sky bridge and skylights create a unique space and flood the home with light.

A pergola extends the home outside.

bright central core and provide additional connection to living areas when desired. An enclosed walk-in dry-storage area is located below the entrance deck and provides ample space for bike storage, tools, and camping gear. Structural exposed peeled-pole columns extend the full two stories, emulating the surrounding forest. Interior finishes are composed of natural materials such as fir beams and flooring, cedar ceilings, and natural stone. Indigenous finish materials complement the wooded site and, true to the bungalow philosophy, connect this home to the surrounding environment.

Main Floor

Bath

Kitchen

Dining
Room

Living
Room

Entry

Home
Office

Bath

Loft

Master
Bath

Bedroom

Closet

Master
Bedroom

Upper Floor

Milwaukee Garlow

Size: 792 sq. ft.

Main floor: 396 sq. ft.

Upper floor: 396 sq. ft.

Designers: Mike and Debbie Schubert

Builders: Vernon Construction, General Contractor;
 Town & Country Contractors

: Snuggled next to a new bungalow within an existing traditional neighborhood, this garlow is just steps from the main house, providing a separation from the automobile and adding the ability to allow light into all sides of the main house. The main floor of the garlow is designed to hold a single small to mid-sized automobile and a bounty of sporting equipment. The single garage door allows for storage along the left side and rear of the garage, while a door at the rear exits to a deck that connects to the main house. The internal staircase is accessed off the deck and leads to a fully finished second floor with bath. The second floor functions as guest quarters, a bonus room, or an at-home office. The addition of a small kitchenette would create a small sophisticated studio apartment that could offset the cost of the garage. Detaching the garage from the main house not only provides alternative uses for the garlow but aids in creating a historic scale in the existing 1920s neighborhood. The use of board-and-batten siding in conjunction with lap siding and vintage window designs sympathetically blends this garlow with its community.

Upper Floor

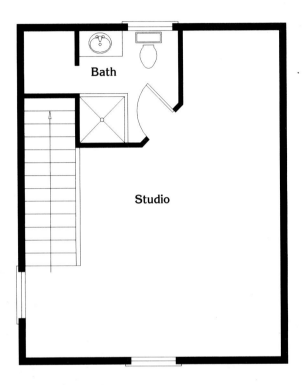

Bath

Studio

Main Floor

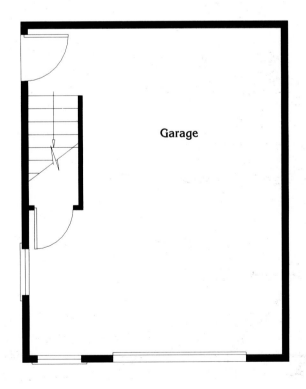

Garage

NorthTown Woods Garlow

Size: 960 sq. ft.
Main floor: 480 sq. ft.
Upper floor: 480 sq. ft.
Designer: The Bungalow Company
Builder: Reese Construction

: DESIGNED AS A PROTOTYPE garage for a new traditional neighborhood, the two-stall garage is twenty-feet wide by twenty-four feet long with a single sixteen-foot-wide garage door. The garage comfortably houses two medium-sized cars and a staircase to the second floor. The second floor is accessed at the rear of the garage with a door to the outside. The second floor contains a full bath and the ability to add a kitchenette. Large shed dormers on the second floor create 480 square feet of living area, which is ample for a cozy rental, nanny quarters, or efficient office for three. Detaching the garlow from the house on a narrow lot and locating the garage toward the rear of the home helps create space between neighbors while using the garage to screen one neighbor's backyard from another's. The longer driveway pushes the parking pad off the

Garlow with color option

street and makes a safe haven for children to ride bikes or play. A detached garage on the lot with slope also provides an opportunity to use steps in the landscape to transition up or down to the house without elevating the home to work with the car. The exterior of the garlow is designed to be flexible and coordinate with the exterior of the main house by scaling down many of the main house details.

Main Floor

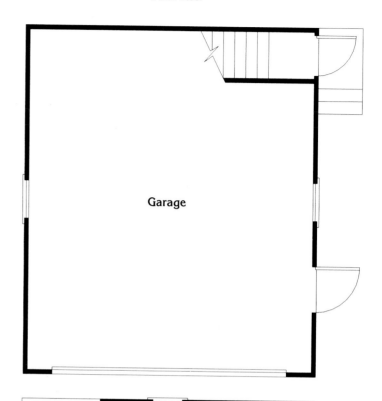

Upper Floor

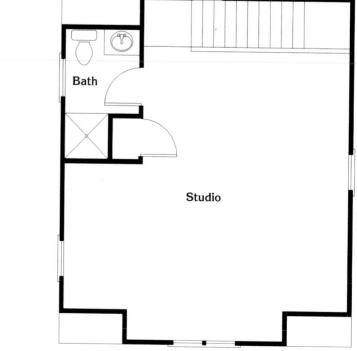

Environmental Concerns

■ ■

: As NATURAL RESOURCES dwindle and the environment is jeopardized by pollution, home builders and buyers must ask what can be done to preserve natural resources and reduce pollution. The answer is not simple, and as new materials are developed, everyday environmental concerns are more difficult to understand. There are many approaches to "environmental building," but focusing on building longevity and conserving natural resources is a good place to start. The reality is that since many homes being built today may not outlive their mortgages, builders and designers must continually evaluate how they are creating buildings and strive to improve building efficiency, longevity, and aesthetics. Building properly detailed homes that will, with maintenance, stand the test of time (200–500 years) is a step in the right direction. Smart design is a key component in creating a long-term environmental solution. Designing homes that take fewer resources to heat and cool over time is an easy way to positively affect the use of resources every day. Proper insulation and siting a home to work with the sun and shade can have a dramatic effect on energy consumption and should be considered on every new home. The best way to stand the test of time is to look at the past and distinguish which details and methods have worked and which have not. The proper detailing for a climate and the correct heating, cooling and ventilation is the backbone of new building longevity. Conservation is a holistic approach; building smaller, more energy-efficient homes on less land and in locations that will reduce the amount of miles driven per year is a solution in which we can all participate.

■ ■

The Cottage

Size: 1,539 sq. ft.
Main floor: 924 sq. ft.
Upper floor: 615 sq. ft.
Designer: Robert W. Knight, AIA

: DESIGNED FOR A BEAUTIFUL HARBOR on the shores of the Maine coast, this shingled cabin speaks the language of its nineteenth-century neighbors. Down East cottages of the past were always very much about porches; however, putting the porches on the south side made these houses very dark. Infilling the porch with living space while maintaining the historical rooflines creates an authentic building form with an updated floor plan.

Carving out a small corner on the southeast side of the house creates an outdoor living space in which to sit on a rainy day or retreat from the intense summer sun. The generous porch on the north side establishes a sense of entry and scale in the home.

Immediately inside the front door is an entry hall with a vaulted ceiling and a staircase to the second floor, where there are two bedrooms tucked under the roof and a single bath. Adjacent to the entry on the main floor is one bedroom and another bath. The main living space of the house is a unified kitchen, dining, and living space. The dining room is built into a bay on the south side of the home; on the east side of the bay is a window, and to the west a low wall separates the room from a small home office. The living room is defined by a furniture grouping focused around the fireplace, with filtered views through the dining room to the outdoors. A large deck makes up the foreground of the plan and grounds the house to a rock ledge that slopes steeply down to the harbor. A hidden storage area under the eaves and individual sinks in the bedrooms encompass all the charm and character of an original Down East cottage.

Upper Floor

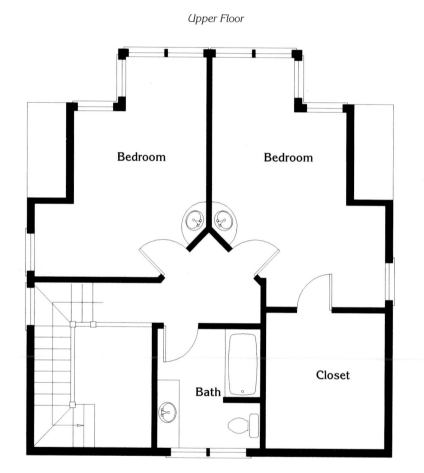

Main Floor

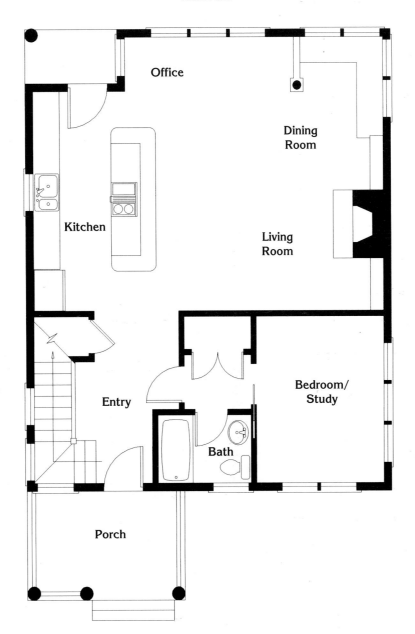

Office

Dining
Room

Kitchen

Living
Room

Entry

Bedroom/
Study

Bath

Porch

CRAFTSMAN GUEST COTTAGES

Size: 232 to 548 sq. ft. on main floor
Designer: John Robinson,
    Robinson Residential Design, Inc.

: SMALL AND SIMPLE BUNGALOW cottages were offered for sale in many of the plan books of the early 1900s as vacation homes and retreats. Reminiscent of original retreat housing, these uniquely designed guesthouses feature covered porches, an abundance of windows, and classic exterior detailing. These simple structures vary from 232 square feet to 548 square feet and are planned as stand-alone cottages or as accessory buildings to a main house. Originally designed for vacationing, the bungalow cottage is finding new success as a detached home office or mother-in-law apartment. In many cities, zoning laws have been revised to allow a second income-generating residence on a single building lot, which is an ideal fit for the bungalow cottage. Increasing urban density has proven an invaluable tool in the prevention of urban sprawl, and building a

Telecommuting is a reality for more people in our modern times, and
a small cottage is the ideal solution for a work environment at home.

Reminiscent of retreat housing, this is a
perfect starter cottage for a vacation getaway.

small cottage that uses few resources to construct and small amounts of energy to main-

tain is a proactive approach to preserving the environment.

Bungalow cottages offer all the comforts of home in a variety of sizes and designs. Options

include lofts, full bathrooms, window seats, dining nooks, and kitchenettes. Exterior style

and detail can be designed to complement the main house. Bungalow cottages are often

built on recreational property to allow owners ample time to site, design, and finance their

primary residence. The bungalow style can be exemplified in cottages of any size; how-

ever, the concept of "less is more" is never clearer than in a bungalow cottage.

Large Cottage

Guest Cottage B

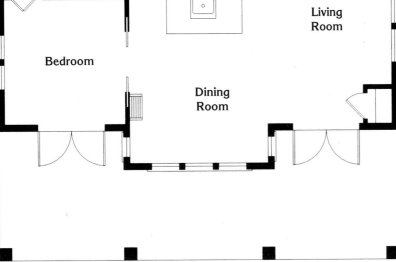

Bath

Kitchen

Living
Room

Bedroom

Dining
Room

Main Floor

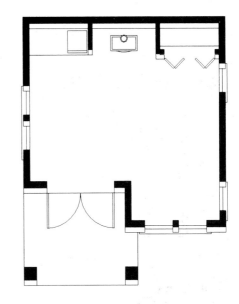

Guest Cottage A

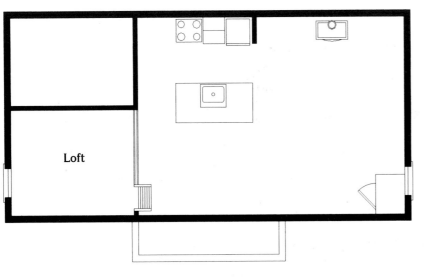

Loft

Upper Floor

Bath

Bobbitt Studio/Garlow

Size: 986 sq. ft.
Main floor: 832 sq. ft.
Garage level: 832 sq. ft.
Designer: Stephen Bobbitt
Builder: Port Blakely Builders

: This multifunctional structure was designed for a wooded hillside overlooking the Puget Sound. It is perched above the owners' full-time residence located on the beach below. Intended to serve as a complement to the main house, it provides a lower-level garage and workshop, with storage lofts for recreational gear suspended above. Upstairs, a simple high-gabled space serves a variety of functions, including a game room and guest quarters with a small kitchen and bathroom, topped by a loft space accessed by a spiral stair, overlooking the game room.

This building stretches vertically to minimize its footprint and site impact among the evergreen trees. The gabled roof form has an archetypal simplicity, clearly expressing the structural logic of its frame. Generous eaves serve to anchor the tall form to the steep site while creating a wide dry zone around the building's perimeter, an important issue in the rainy climate. Large windows on three sides provide views into the trees and out to the water, while washing the interior with the softly diffused light of the forest. On the downhill side, a small balcony serves as a viewing platform suspended high above the ground, a treehouse-like appendage from which to survey the surroundings.

Materials were selected to link the structure to its site and provide a low-maintenance cladding. The weathering process, creating an organic structural skin, that is the architectural equivalent of tree bark, enhances these. The interiors refine this concept, utilizing natural fir cabinetry and trim, a cedar-plank ceiling, and drawing inspiration from the forest palette for color

selections in upholstery fabrics and floor coverings.

Main Floor

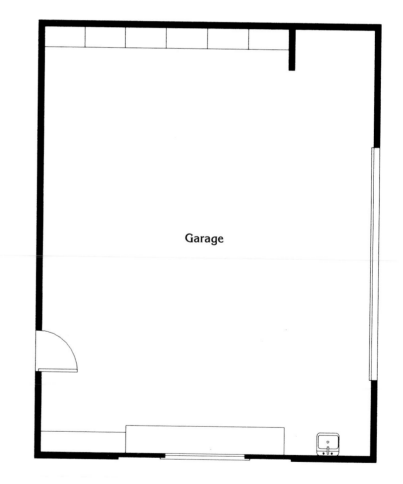

Garage

Second Floor

Third Floor

Bath

Recreation
Room

Storage

Loft

Open to
below

Ultimate Bungalows:
Views & Vistas

: Ultimate bungalows exemplify the union of craftsmanship, materials, and building form. The homes contained within this section share the philosophy inspired by Greene & Greene architects in the design and production of the nine masterworks that defined the ultimate bungalows. Celebrating their connection to nature, ultimate bungalows convey the harmony that can take place between things man-made and nature. Appearing to grow from the landscape, the building takes its place in nature; as the seasons change and time passes, the use of indigenous materials and colors fuses the building with the site, creating a marriage of building and site. A far cry from the humble production bungalows of the 1920s, the ultimate bungalow has served as a principal to guide the intentions of designers and craftsmen in their everyday pursuit of excellence and integrity.

■ ■

THE SONORA

Size: 2,005 sq. ft.
Main floor: 1,333 sq. ft.
Upper floor: 672 sq. ft.
Attached garage: 484 sq. ft.
Detached garage: 936 sq. ft.
Main-floor workshop: 504 sq. ft
Upper-floor studio: 432 sq. ft.
Designers: Middleton Design; Mike and Robyn Knoell
Builders: Mike and Robyn Knoell

: MIKE AND ROBYN HAVE BEEN FANS of the bungalow style for years. After restoring a number of bungalows themselves, they decided to embark on crafting a reproduction bungalow. Frustrated with current reproductions of the style, they collaborated with designer Mike Middleton to create an ultimate airplane bungalow reproduction. Mike and Robyn, who worked as general contractors on the project, took extra care during the design process to develop a design that would harmonize with the site and, in the sprit of Charles and Henry Greene, appear as if the home had grown from the land.

The airplane bungalow is most often identified by the "cockpit," which is a raised second-level living space with four independent walls. Characteristically, the roof line of the airplane

A beautifully detailed fireplace and built-in bookcases are the finishing touches of any bungalow living room.

home transcends time and creates a clear vision of an original airplane bungalow. The use of indigenous stone on the wood-burning fireplace connects the home with the local environment. Boxed beams, reproduction lighting, and authentically styled cabinetry were all carefully researched and executed to reinforce the bungalow lineage. The detached garage with the mother-in-law apartment above is a

bungalow is shallow in pitch and the roof overhangs cantilever three to four feet from the line of the building, giving the home a winged appearance. The Knoells were vigilant in their attention to interior detailing, using authentically scaled and proportioned finish treatments and spaces. The

departure from the original building form; however, with a clear understanding of the bungalow-design vocabulary, the apartment evolved as an essential element of the project. The carriage-style garage doors respond to the scale and detail of the home's true divided-light windows. Placement of the garage at the rear of the site has focused attention on the main house and de-emphasized the role of the garage on the architecture.

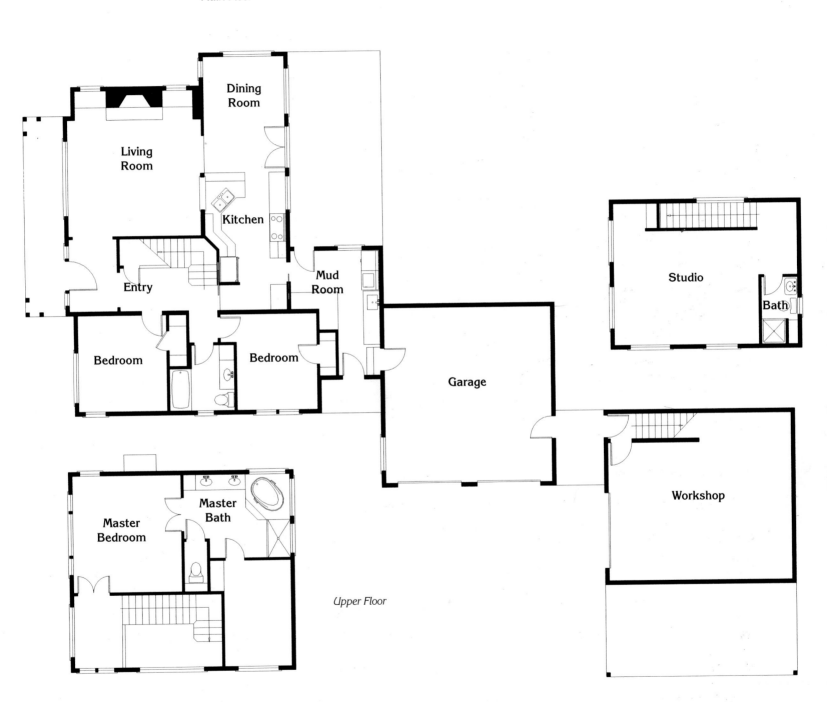

Main Floor

Dining
Room

Living
Room

Kitchen

Entry

Mud
Room

Bedroom

Bedroom

Garage

Studio

Bath

Workshop

Upper Floor

Master
Bath

Master
Bedroom

PHILLIPS RESIDENCE

Size: 4,007 sq. ft.
Main floor: 2,916 sq. ft.
Lower floor: 1,091 sq. ft.
Detached garage: 576 sq. ft.
Designer: David Balas, AIA
Builder: Craftsman Building, Stephen Deines

: THE CLIENT BROUGHT to this project a list of requirements gleaned from Christopher Alexander's book, *A Pattern Language*, and a memory of Pasadena from his boyhood in California. After moving with his wife and two sons from Hawaii to the Northwest, he hoped to recapture the details and spirit of the Greene brothers, Frank Lloyd Wright, and Japanese architecture.

The site is steeply sloping, with a 180-degree view of the Olympic Mountains, bounded by a forest preserve at both ends. The lot is long and narrow, and short-platted for two homes. This first house needed to remain low to preserve the views from the upper lot. The house was to be sold as a spec house, and the proceeds used to build a complementary house on the upper lot. Though this never happened, it shaped

houses, and used in everything from garage details to fireplace tools. Lighting from Arroyo Craftsman and Rejuvenation was used throughout. Mahogany kitchen cabinets were faithfully replicated from those in the Gamble House kitchen. Doors and windows were painstakingly copied from originals—the front door in tripartite design is based on the one from the Gamble House, but simplified and without the stained glass. The lookout tower room with exposed cedar beams and operating awning windows was inspired by the Washington fire tower that served as Jack Kerouac's writing loft one summer.

the design of the Phillips house. The roof is long and sheltering, with forty-two-inch eaves and a fiberglass-reinforced bitumen roof, including temple uplifts at roof gables, which mimic the Greenes' use of "Malthoid Sheet Roofing." Details were researched from the Pratt, Blacker, and Gamble

Public and private wings are angled away from the central hall, the front entry aligning with three French doors that open onto a sheltered veranda facing the view. The loggia functions to protect inhabitants from the swift breezes flowing up from the valley below. The living room's proportions were inspired by Wright's "Wingspread" in Wisconsin. Two ancient slabs of mountain cedar held by forged brackets surround the bronze iron-spot brick fireplace.

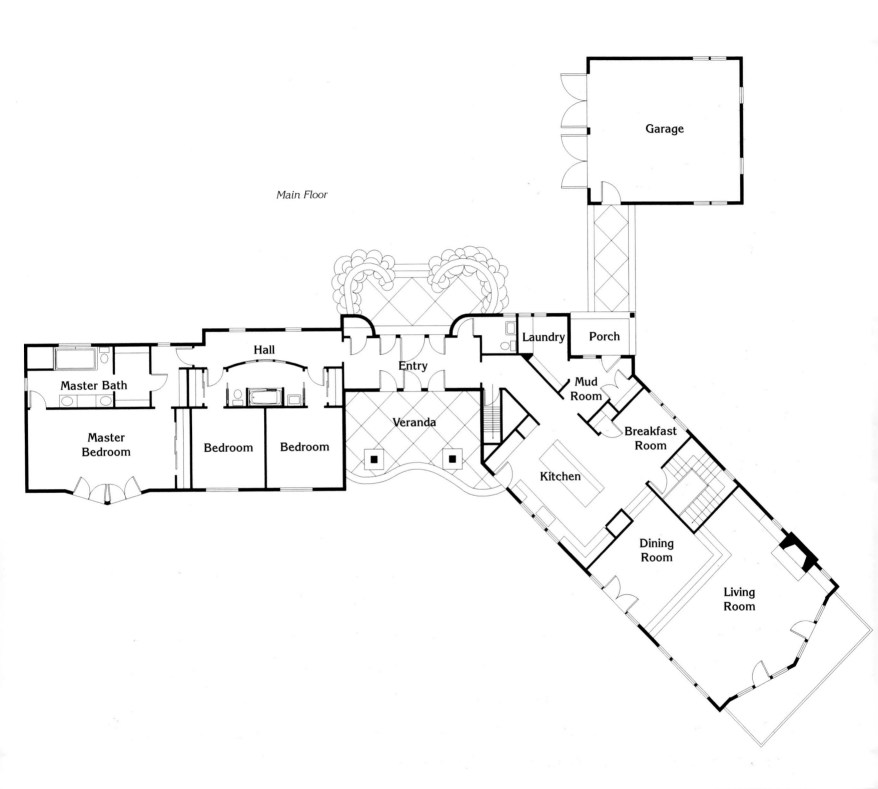

Main Floor

Garage

Laundry

Porch

Entry

Hall

Master Bath

Mud Room

Master Bedroom

Bedroom

Bedroom

Veranda

Kitchen

Breakfast Room

Dining Room

Living Room

WINTHROP HOUSE

Size: 2,650 sq. ft.
Main floor: 2,056 sq. ft.
Upper Floor: 594 sq. ft.
Designers: Stock & Associates,
  Steve Erickson and Shelly Stock;
  Integrated Design Concepts,
  Howard Cherrington, design consultant
Builder: A. J. & Company Construction, Inc.

: AFTER YEARS OF RENTING homes a week at a time as a getaway in the beautiful Methow Valley of eastern Washington, Mark and Karen Endresen decided that it was time to build a retreat they could call their own. The site the owners selected was at the crest of a hill on a forty-acre parcel overlooking the town of Winthrop. To minimize the impact of a large house on such a prominent location, the designers organized the living spaces on one level, which is angled to follow the curve of the hill and maximize the panoramic views of the Methow Valley below and the North Cascade mountain range beyond.

The house is divided into three parts. Visitors enter via a hall that bisects the house and connects to the vistas through glass doors at either end. A vaulted great room both separates and

128

The vaulted ceiling of this open kitchen, dining, and living room is made cozier with the addition of beams.

stone fireplace and chimney anchors one end of the great room and contains the cooking, eating, and major gathering activities. French doors on either side open onto outdoor terraces formed of the same stone as the fireplace.

The owners admired the early-twentieth-century designs of the Greene brothers in California. While their budget did not allow an exact replication of the intricate detailing of these homes, the Endresens asked that the design of their new home reflect the spirit of the brothers' architecture. With this in mind, quarter-sawn oak millwork is carefully coordinated with a warm palette of ochre and green paint colors to maximize the overall impact.

functions as the meeting point for the more private master bedroom to the west and the guest quarters at the east end of the house. A generous field-

Additionally, custom designed casework, leaded glass, and light fixtures are incorporated throughout the house to achieve the integrated design associated with the Arts & Crafts era.

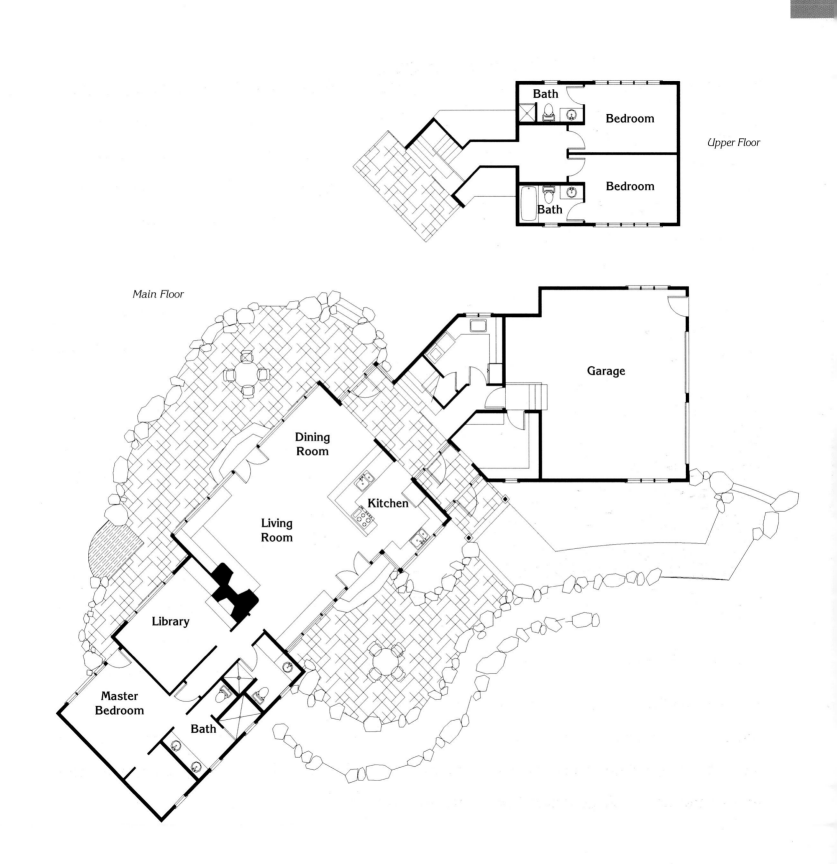

Upper Floor

Bath

Bedroom

Bedroom

Bath

Main Floor

Dining Room

Garage

Living Room

Kitchen

Library

Master Bedroom

Bath

The Agate Pass

Size: 3,007 sq. ft.
Main floor: 1,916 sq. ft.
Lower floor: 1,091 sq. ft.
Attached garage: 576 sq. ft.
Designer: David Balas
Builder: Craftsman Building, Stephen Deines

: KIM AND ROB WILLIAMSON chose to site their home nestled on a high bluff overlooking Agate Passage on Puget Sound. They brought memories of Oregon coast bungalows and their dream of a cozy but spacious home to this outcropping. Making the most of a dramatic site, this house has three faces—main elevations exist to the east, south, and west, each carefully composed to appear both dynamic and peacefully ordered.

The original cabin on this challenging site, cobbled together in the 1940s, was perched precariously on the cliff. Before its final demolition, it provided living quarters for the owners' family during construction. Concrete foundation walls remain to create a terraced garden leading to the beach. The original property owners collected rare rhododendrons, which were moved to

The more compact homes of the Greene brothers, such as the Jennie Reeve House (1903) and the Emma Black House (1904) inspired the Williamsons' use of a flowing plan with intimate spaces linked by axial views. The main entry, recessed into the front of the house, opens onto a panoramic view seen through a plaster archway. Street-side rooms look through broad openings and framed interior vignettes to the water beyond. The formal dining room is glassed in on three sides and sits between two open porches, leading to the living room and kitchen respectively. A breakfast booth with a corner window beckons in the kitchen. The mud room is accessed from two sides and is down a level to eliminate mud and sand being tracked into the house. The sloping site afforded the design of two basement bedrooms with water views. Up the main stair is the master suite, which includes an office with a feature fireplace and the bedroom. Between the two, over the dining room, is a veranda sleeping porch, offering a third covered porch on the northwest elevation.

a forested part of the site during construction. They have landscaped the new house to provide a feeling of permanence and belonging.

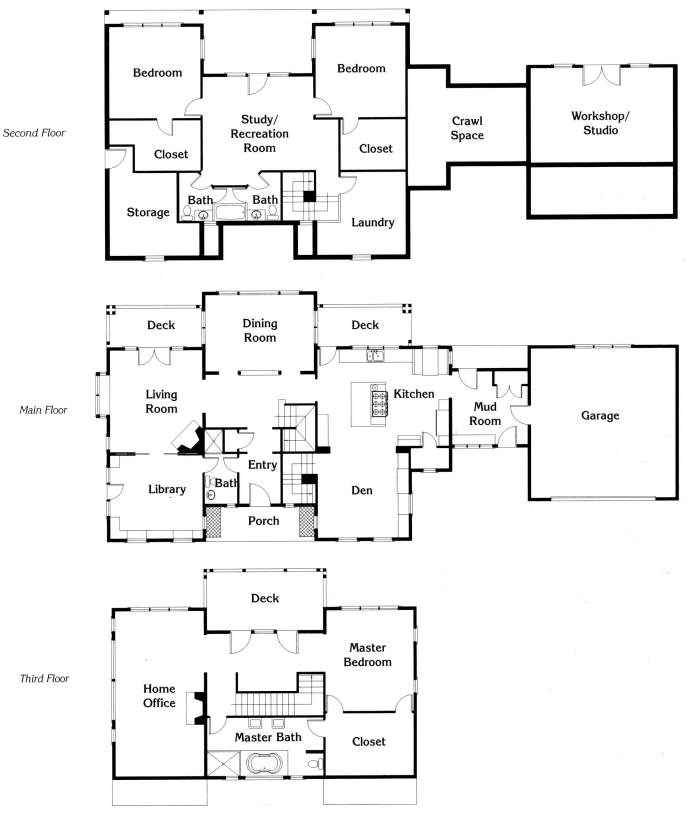

Second Floor

Bedroom

Bedroom

Study/
Recreation
Room

Crawl
Space

Workshop/
Studio

Closet

Closet

Storage

Bath

Bath

Laundry

Main Floor

Deck

Dining
Room

Deck

Living
Room

Kitchen

Mud
Room

Garage

Entry

Library

Bath

Den

Porch

Third Floor

Deck

Master
Bedroom

Home
Office

Master Bath

Closet

RESOURCES
DESIGNERS, ARCHITECTS & BUILDERS

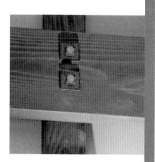

Accessories

Liberty Valance & Curtain
782 N. Fair Oaks Avenue
Pasadena, CA 91103
(877) WADI ROD
www.libertyvalances.com

Trimbelle River Studio & Design
P.O. Box 568
Ellsworth, WI 54011
(715) 273-4844
www.trimbelleriver.com

Associations

Environment Building News —Building Green, Inc.
122 Birge Street, Suite 30
Brattleboro, VT 05301
(802) 257-7300
www.buildinggreen.com

National Association of Home Builders
1201 Fifteenth Street NW
Washington DC 20005
(800) 368-5242
(202) 266-8200 DC area only
www.nahb.com

Cabinets

Crown Point Cabinets
153 Charlestown Road
Claremont, NH 03743
(800) 999-4994
www.crown-point.com

Designers

Ashmore/Kessenich Design
6336 NE Garfield Avenue
Portland, OR 97211
(503) 286-6258

The Bungalow Company
P.O. Box 584
Bend, OR 97709
(541) 312-2674
www.thebungalowcompany.com

Cottage Designs
1293 NW Wall Street #1391
Bend, OR 97701
(541) 383-9015
www.cottagedesigns.com

David Balas Architect
5173 Eagle Harbor Drive NE
Bainbridge Island, WA 98110
(206) 842-9093
www.davidbalasarchitect.com

Eric Lewtas Architect
32 Pickering Farm Road
Hancock, NH 03449
(603) 525-9406

Knight Associates, Architects Lucia's Little Houses
157 Hinckley Ridge Road
Blue Hill, ME 04614-0803
(207) 374-2845
info@knightarchitect.com

Middleman Design & Drafting
1627 NE Third, Suite 4
Bend, OR 97701
(541) 383-0633

Robert Moore Architect
8427 Fletcher Bay Road
Bainbridge Island, WA 98110
(206) 842-6366
rmoore@robertmoorearch.com

Robinson Residential Design Inc.
30 Lake Street
Regina, SK S4S 4A8
Canada
(306) 586-5950
www.robinsonplans.com

Scott Gilbride Architect
1685 NW Fourth Street
Bend, OR 97701
(541) 388-3768
www.scottgilbride.com

Stephen Bobbitt Architects
109 Bell Street
Seattle, WA 98121
(206) 728-4400
www.srbarch.com

Stock & Associates
109 Bell Street
Seattle, WA 98121
(206) 443-0494
www.stockandassociates.com

Wenzlau Architects
900 Winslow Way East, Suite 150
Bainbridge Island, WA 98110
(206) 780-6882
charlie@wenzlau-architects.com

Engineered Lumber

American Plywood Association
P.O. Box 11700
Tacoma, WA 98411-0700
(253) 565-6600
www.apawood.org

Boise Cascade Corp.
P.O. Box 50
Boise, ID 83728
(208) 384-6161
www.boisecascade.com

Simpson Strong Tie
4120 Dublin Boulevard
Suite 400
Dublin, CA 94568
(925) 560-9000
www.strongtie.com

Trus Joist (TJI)
200 E. Mallard Drive
Boise, ID 83706
(800) 338-0515
www.tjm.com

Western Woods Products Association (WWPA)
522 SW Fifth Avenue, Suite 500
Portland, OR 97204-2122
(503) 224-3930
www.wwpa.org

Fireplaces

Buckley Rumford Co.
1035 Monroe Street
Port Townsend, WA 98368
(360) 385-9974
www.rumford.com

Chimney Pot Shoppe
Michael Bentley Enterprises
Avella, PA 15312
(724) 345-3601
www.chimmeypotshoppe.com

FireSpaces
223 NW Ninth Avenue
Portland, OR 97209
(503) 227-0547
www.firespaces.com

Flooring

Armstrong—DLW Linoleum
www.armstrong.com

Emerson Hardwood Floors/Cross Cut Hardwoods
www.emersonhardwood.com

TimberGrass LLC
7995 NE Day Road
Bainbridge Island, WA 98110
(800) 929-6333
www.timbergrass.com

Garage Doors

Designer Doors
183 E. Pomeroy Street
River Falls, WI 54022
(715) 426-1100
(800) 241-0525
www.designerdoors.com

Hahn's Wood Working Company Inc.
181 Meister Avenue
Branchburg, NJ 08876
(908) 793-1415
www.hahnswoodworking.com

Hardware

The Bungalow Gutter Bracket Co.
P.O. Box 22144
Lexington, KY 40522-2144
(859) 335-1555
www.bungalowgutterbracket.com

Chown Hardware
333 NW Sixteenth Avenue
Portland, OR 97209
(503) 243-6500
(800) 547-1930
www.chown.com

Craftsman Hardware
Arlington, WA 98223
(360) 403-7202
www.craftsmanhardware.com

Craftsmen Hardware Company, Ltd.
P.O. Box 161
Marceline, MO 64658
(660) 376-2481
www.craftsmenhardware.com

Crown City Hardware
1047 N. Allen Avenue
Pasadena, CA 91104-3298
(626) 794-1188 local
(626) 794-0234 catalog direct
(800) 950-1047 orders only
www.crowncityhardware.com

EmTek Decorative Hardware
(800) 356-2741
www.emtekproducts.com

Inserts & Stoves

Heat & Glow
20802 Kensington Boulevard
Lakeville, MN 55044
(888) 743-2887
www.heatnglo.com

Vermont Castings
410 Admiral Boulevard
Mississauga, ON L5T 2N6
Canada
(800) 227-8683
www.vermontcastings.com

Interior and Exterior Doors

Buffelen Woodworking Company
1901 Taylor Way
Tacoma, WA 98421
(253) 627-1191
www.ep.org

Great Northwest Storm & Screen Door Company
11145 – 120th Avenue NE
Kirkland, WA 98033
(800) 895-3667
(425) 827-4595
www.greatnwdoors.com

International Door & Latch
191 Seneca Road
P.O. Box 25755
Eugene, OR 97402
(541) 686-5647
www.internationaldoor.com

Nord
300 W. Marine View Drive
Everett, WA 98201-1030
(800) 900-NORD
(425) 259-9292
www.norddoor.com

Simpson Door Company
400 Simpson Avenue
McCleary, WA 98557
(800) 952-4057
www.simpsondoor.com

Interior Finish Material

Environmental Home Center
1724 Fourth Avenue South
Seattle, WA 98134
(800) 281-9785
www.built-e.com

Shelter Supply, Inc.
17725 Juniper Path
Lakeville, MN 55044
(800) 762-8399
www.sheltersupply.com

Sierra Pine
West Coast Sales
Roseville, CA 95661
(800) 676-3339
www.sierrapine.com

Interior Furnishings

The Craftsman Home
3048 Claremont Avenue
Berkeley, CA 94705
(510) 655-6503
www.craftsmanhome.com

The Craftsman Homes Connection
(509) 535-5098
www.crafthome.com

L. & J. G. Stickley, Inc.
One Stickley Drive
P.O. Box 480
Manlius, NY 13104-0480
(315) 682-5500
www.stickley.com

Michael FitzSimmons Decorative Arts
311 W. Superior Street
Chicago, IL 60610
(312) 787-0496
www.fitzdecarts.com

WILLOWGLEN.COM
351 Willow Street
San Jose, CA 95110-3223
(408) 293-2284
www.willowglen.com

Lighting

Craftsmen Lighting by Craftsmen Hardware Company, Ltd.
P.O. Box 161
Marceline, MO 64658
(660) 376-2481
www.craftsmenhardware.com

Historic Lighting
114 E. Lemon Avenue
Old Town Monrovia, CA 91016
(626) 303-4899
www.historiclighting.com

Luminaria Lighting
154 S. Madison Street
Spokane, WA 99201
(800) 638-5619
www.luminarialighting.com

Old California Lantern Company
975 N. Enterprise Street
Orange, CA 92867
(800) 577-6679
www.oldcalifornia.com

Rejuvenation Lamp & Fixture Company
2550 NW Nicolai Street
Portland, OR 97210
(888) 401-1900
www.rejuvenation.com

Periodicals

American Bungalow
P.O. Box 756
123 S. Baldwin Avenue
Sierra Madre, CA 91024
(800) 350-3363
www.ambungalow.com

Fine Homebuilding
The Taunton Press
63 S. Main Street
P.O. Box 5506
Newtown, CT 06470-5506
(206) 426-8171
www.finehomebuilding.com

The Journal of Light Construction
186 Allen Brooke Lane
Williston, VT 05495
(802) 879-3335
www.jlconline.com

Period Homes Magazine
69A Seventh Avenue
Brooklyn, NY 11217
(718) 636-0788
www.period-homes.com

Style 1900
333 N. Main Street
Lambertville, NJ 08530
(609) 397-9374
www.ragoarts.com

Plumbing

A-ball Plumbing
1703 W. Burnside Street
Portland, OR 97209
(800) 228-0134
www.a-ball.com

Flood Saver
P.O. Box 1782
Stanwood, WA 98292
(360) 629-9269
www.floodsaver.com

Kohler
444 Highland Drive
Kohler, WI 53044
(920) 457-4441
www.kohler.com

Siding/Trim

Bear Creek Lumber
P.O. Box 669
Winthrop, WA 98862
(800) 597-7191
www.bearcreeklumber.com

Cedar Shake & Shingle Bureau
P.O. Box 1178
Sumas, WA 98295-1178
(604) 820-7700
www.cedarbureau.org

James Hardie
26300 La Alameda Drive
Suite 250
Mission Viejo, CA 92691
(888) JHARDIE
www.jameshardie.com

Lakeside Lumber
17850 SW Boones Ferry Road
Lake Oswego, OR 97035
(503) 635-3693
www.lakesidelumber.com

Tile

Motawi Tile Works
170 Enterprise Drive
Ann Arbor, MI 48103
(734) 213-0017
www.motawi.com

Norberry Tile
207 Second Avenue South
Seattle, WA 98104
(206) 343-9916
www.norberrytile.com

Tile Restoration Center
3511 Interlake North
Seattle, WA 98103
(206) 633-4866
www.tilerestorationcenter.com

Windows

Eagle Window and Door of Washington
11807 Northcreek Parkway
Suite B-102
Bothell, WA 98011
(425) 482-0178
www.eaglewindows.com

Marvin Windows & Doors
www.marvin.com

Milgard Windows
www.milgard.com

Pozzi Wood Windows
62845 Boyd Acres Road
Bend, OR 97701
(541) 382-4411
(800) 547-6880
www.pozzi.com